Three Plays
on
Wisconsin History

John Nicholas Schweitzer

Contents

3

4

Preface

These plays were performed by community theater groups in southern Wisconsin: <u>Fighting Bob</u> in Madison in 1998, <u>Sergeant Bates</u> in Stoughton and Edgerton in 2003, and <u>Surrounded by Reality</u> in Madison in 2006. All three incorporated music to some degree, which is not included here.

<u>Fighting Bob: A Love Story</u> is a musical biography of the life of Robert La Follette and his wife, Belle Case La Follette. "Fighting Bob" La Follette was a gifted orator, a lawyer, Dane County District Attorney, U.S. Congressman from Wisconsin, Governor, U.S. Senator, and Presidential candidate on the Progressive ticket in 1924. Belle La Follette was a lawyer, an editor, a syndicated columnist, a regular Chatauqua speaker, and active in the suffrage movement and other women's causes.

<u>The Saga of Sergeant Bates</u> is a dramatization of the true story of Sergeant Gilbert Bates, who served in the First Wisconsin Heavy Artillery during the Civil War and who, three years later, walked unarmed from Vicksburg across Mississippi, Alabama, Georgia, South Carolina, North Carolina and Virginia to Washington, carrying the Stars and Stripes to win a bet in which he asserted that the Southerners were not still hostile to the North. Songs of the times are used throughout, sometimes as curtain music and sometimes as integral parts of the scenes.

<u>Surrounded by Reality</u> is a full-length play on the history of Madison, Wisconsin, commissioned by Historic Madison, Inc. for the city's sesquicentennial in 2006. It

consists of four scenes, set in 1862, 1883, 1922, and 1963, with three continuity devices:

First, each story centers on a different generation of the same family, the Atwoods, starting with David Atwood, the first editor of the *Wisconsin State Journal*.

Second, the four major scenes are linked by an extended and fractured scene depicting the modern-day descendants of the Atwood family, especially the family's daughter who unearths old family photos and letters from the attic.

Third, each generation deals with an issue of prejudice against a different group, which had been largely assimilated by the next scene.

Fighting Bob - A Love Story

Book by John Nicholas Schweitzer
Music by Taras Nahirniak

As performed by the Madison Theatre Guild
June 12-20, 1998

7

Summary of Acts and Scenes

Act 1.

Scene 1: *Fighting Bob's Funeral - Part 1* (1925)
    Setting: the U.S. Senate chamber
    Cast: chorus
                Belle Case La Follette (age 66)
                Supreme Court Justice Louis Brandeis
                (audience members)
                Fola La Follette (age from 24 to 88)
    Musical Numbers: 1. Requiem for Fighting
                                  Bob
                        2. If (solo setting)

Scene 2: *The Governor's Holiday Ball - Part 1*
                (1905)
    Setting: the Governor's mansion, decorated for
             Christmas
    Cast: Robert Marion La Follette ("Bob") (age
                50)
                La Follette children: Fola (age 24),
                      Robert Jr. (age 11), Philip (age
                      9), and Mary (age 7)
                Belle (age 46)
    Musical Numbers: 3. The Land of Milk and
                                    Honey
                      4. The Land of Milk and
                                  Honey - Reprise

Scene 3: *The Blue Savage* (1867)
    Setting: a farmyard with packing crates
    Cast: Bob (age 12)
                Bob's sister Josephine (age 14)
                Other children and pets

8

Bob's mother Mary (about 49)
Fola

Musical Numbers: 5. Circus Music
                     6. Horizons on the Prairie

Scene 4: *College and Belle* (1878)
    Setting: the office of the <u>University Press</u> at the
            University of Wisconsin
    Cast: Bob (age 23)
            Students 1 and 2
            Belle (age 19)
            Fola
    Musical Numbers: 7. How Do I Choose?
                         8. Who Tells Me What I
                                 Should Be?
                         9. Reprise of 7 & 8

Scene 5: *La Follette and La Follette* (1883)
    Setting: the Dane County District Attorney's
            office
    Cast: Attorney
            Bob (age 28)
            Belle (age 24)
            Fola
    Musical Number: 10. Partners

Scene 6: *Politics and Money* (1891)
    Setting: the Plankinton House (Hotel) in
            Milwaukee
    Cast: Politicians and business leaders
            Citizens (dancers and others)
            Senator Philetus Sawyer
            Bob (age 36)
    Musical Numbers: 11. The Lobyists' Waltz
                         12. Monopolies Grow and

9

Profits Flow
13. The Game

Act 2.

Scene 7: *The Governor's Holiday Ball - Part 2*
(1905)
Setting: the Governor's mansion, decorated for
Christmas
Cast: Bob (age 50)
LaFollette children: Fola (age 24),
Robert Jr. (age 11), Philip (age
9), and Mary (age 7)
Belle (age 46)
John Ringling
Man 1 & Woman 1, Man 2, Man 3 or
Woman 2
Zona Gale
John Bascom
Citizens (dancers and others)
(audience members)
Musical Numbers: 14. Party Dance
15. Christmas Spirit

Scene 8: *Mr. La Follette Goes to Washington* (1917)
Setting: the U.S. Senate
Cast: Senators 1, 2 & 3
Bob (age 62)
Senator Lane
President of the Senate
Robert, Jr. (age 22)
Fola
Musical Numbers: 16. War
17. I Stand Alone
18. I Stand Alone - Reprise

10

Scene 9: *La Follette for President* (1924)
    Setting: a campaign headquarters
    Cast: Campaign workers
             Men 1, 2 & 3
             Women 1 & 2
             Jane Addams (age 64)
             Belle (age 65)
             Bob (age 69)
             Fola
    Musical Numbers: 19. Can You See Despair?
                            20. Fightin' Bob, The
                                People's Choice
                            21. I Live My Life for Both
                                of You

Scene 10: *Belle and Bob* (1924)
    Setting: a bedroom in the La Follette home
    Cast: Belle (age 65)
             Fola (age 31)
             Bob (age 69)
    Musical Number: 22. Bob and Belle

Scene 11: *Fighting Bob's Funeral - Part 2* (1925)
    Setting: the U.S. Senate chamber
    Cast: chorus
             Belle (age 66)
             Supreme Court Justice Louis Brandeis
    Musical Numbers: 23. If (choral setting)
                            24. Curtain Music

11

ACT 1

Scene 1: Fighting Bob's Funeral - Part 1

[The stage is dark as the curtain goes up. As the chorus begins to sing, the lights come up to semi-darkness. The chorus is standing with its backs to the audience, some carrying umbrellas. Justice Brandeis is standing on a raised podium, but not in the speaker's position. In the middle of the peice, Belle and Fola enter. Belle goes to the speaker's position and is lighted.]

> Musical Number 1: (Brief) Requiem for Fighting Bob
> From the clamor of life,
> From the battles of life,
> From the war against war,
>
> You, a lover of peace,
> You, crusader for peace,
> Rest now in peace, rest now in peace.
> Amen.

Belle: President Coolidge, Vice-President Dawes, Justices of the Supreme Court, Senators, Congressmen, Ladies and Gentlemen. We have assembled here today to honor the memory of an extraordinary man, my husband, Robert Marion La Follette, Senior. It is my privilege to welcome a dear friend to give the funeral oration, a person who needs no introduction to this assemblage, Supreme Court Justice Louis Brandeis.

Brandeis: Thank you. Colleagues, elected officials, and electors, including those among you who until five years ago were kept from being electors solely by reason of your

12

gender. This occasion which brings us together is both sad and happy. We mourn a great man's passing, and we celebrate his life. I speak to you with solemnity; I also speak to you with -- I hope -- some of the humor with which Bob La Follette was well-supplied. I consider myself lucky to have known Bob La Follette. One of his most notable traits was his ability to hold an audience's attention for hours on end. I hasten to assure you that I will not compete with him in that arena.

I am not a great public speaker, as he was. Was. Yes, he is gone now. His passing leaves a great void in our public life. No man in public life expressed the ideals of American Democracy so fully as did Robert LaFollette in his thought, in his acts, and in his life, and no man in public life did so much toward the attainment of those ideals. He inspired us and instructed us in the ideals of democracy as no other man ever did.

He fought many lonely battles, and far too often he was a lonely crusader. He fought and won many of his battles, especially those he waged against corruption and privilege in political life. He fought and lost a few of his battles, most notably to keep us out of the Great War and then to oppose an unjust peace on the vanquished which can only lead to further disaster in Europe. Nevertheless, no matter how much they may have hated what he stood for, there is not one of his enemies who can impugn his character or his courage. He was a man of unimpeachable integrity and unassailable courage.

I said a moment ago that his passing will leave a great void in our public life. It goes without saying that his passing will leave an equally great void in the private lives of his widow and children. I would like to acknowledge their presence here today, especially that of Senator La Follette's widow, Belle Case La Follette. I understand, Mrs. La Follette, that you have been offered your husband's vacant seat in the Senate. Should you choose to accept it, even though no woman has ever sat here, I know that you will be welcomed and that you will grace and honor the seat by your presence. Given your past record of public involvement in causes of great moment, I would expect you to cause just as much trouble here as your husband did.

There's a poem by Rudyard Kipling which has been a source of inspiration to many of us, and I know of no other man who fits it as well as Robert La Follette: If you can keep your head while all around you are losing theirs and blaming it on you ...

[Fola is lighted as she begins to take over the poem from Brandeis. She then comes forward through the crowd and the others leave the stage. Lights/curtain down behind her.]

<u>Musical Number 2: If (solo setting)</u>
If you can keep your head while all around you
      Are losing theirs and blaming it on you,
If you can trust yourself when all men doubt you,
      But make allowances for their doubting, too;

If you can wait and not be tired by waiting,
      Or being lied about, don't deal in lies,
Or being hated, don't give way to hating,
      And yet don't look too good, nor talk too
      wise;
If you can dream -- and not make dreams your
      master;
      If you can think -- and not make thoughts
      your aim;

14

If you can meet with Triumph and Disaster
      And treat those two imposters just the same;

If you can bear to hear the truth you've spoken
      Twisted by knaves to make a trap for fools,
Or watch the things you gave your life to, broken,
      And stoop and build 'em up with worn-out
      tools;

Yours is the Earth and everything that's in it,
      And -- which is more -- you'll be a Man,
      You'll be a Man, my son, you'll be a Man.

Fola: My father was quite a man. My mother was quite a woman, too, but no, she didn't take Dad's seat in the Senate. I always wish she had. Instead, my younger brother Bobbie did. I'm Fola, Fola La Follette. Quite a name, don't you think? I'm proud of it, but it is a little much at times. I can never forget for a minute whose daughter I am. But then, I wouldn't want to forget, because, in addition to being very successful public figures, Bob and Belle La Follette were wonderful parents. They respected their children as they respected each other. And what's more, they had fun with their children as they had fun with each other.

My fondest memories of them are always just around the corner. They loved us children the same way they loved each other, wholeheartedly and enthusiastically. I was the oldest, thirteen years older than Bobbie, and then came Phil and Mary. One of my favorite memories is the last holiday ball we had when Dad was Governor of Wisconsin, in 1905 just before he left for Washington to be a Senator.

[Bobbie, Phil and Mary run on chasing each other around, and then Fola joins the chase. Lights/curtain up.]

15

Fola: I'm gonna get you!

Scene 2: The Governor's Holiday Ball - Part 1

[The children are running and yelling.]

Mary: Papa, Papa!

[Bob enters.]

Bob: Hurry, children. The guests'll be here soon. Fola, you do look lovely. Have I told you how happy I am just to see you again?

Fola: Yes, Papa, only about ten times since I arrived yesterday.

Bob: Well, I say it every time I feel it, and that's every time I see you. We miss you here. I'm sure New York is a fine town, especially for theater, but it is far away.

Fola: It's a wonderful town for theater, and our show is doing well, but my part in this one isn't very big, so it was easy to cover for me for a week, and I simply couldn't miss our last holiday ball.

[Bobbie, Phil and Mary run in. Mary hugs Bob first and then Fola. The boys hug Fola first and then Bob.]

Bobbie: How's this, Do I look all right? **Phil:** Hi Daddy! Hi Fola! **Mary:** Fola! I like your dress!

Bob: Did you see your mother?

Bobbie: She's coming.

[Mary goes to the doorway.]

17

Bob: Are you ready to sing the song we made up for her?

Fola, Bobbie, Phil and Mary: Yes!

Bob: Where's my guitar.

Fola: Right here. [She picks up the guitar and gives it to Bob.] You know, soon I won't be far away at all. When you get to Washington, I'll visit often. [Bobbie, Phil and Mary wail.] What's wrong.

Mary: You'll be near Mama and Papa. We won't.

Bob: Until we get settled, and decide whether Washington will be a good place for them, we've decided they'll all stay here.

Fola: Where.

Bobbie: At a boarding school!

Bob: You know it, the Hillside Home School.

Fola: Oh, the one run by Jane and Ellen Lloyd Jones.

Phil: They're related to that architect, the eccentric one.

Fola: Frank Lloyd Wright? I'm sure he won't be teaching you, unless you decide to study architecture. You'll be all right.

Mary: She's coming!

[Belle enters.]

Belle: The guests are starting to arrive.

[Bob plays at least a chord, following which the orchestra can enter.]

Musical Number 3: The Land of Milk and Honey

The land of milk and honey calls
to me wheree'er I roam
of prairies, lakes and waterfalls:
my dear Wisconsin home.

This land where all are truly free
beneath the sky's blue dome,
where families live in harmony:
my dear Wisconsin home,
my dear Wisconsin home,
my dear Wisconsin home.

Belle: What a marvelous family we have.

Bobbie: We have another verse we just made up, while we were upstairs.

Bob: Oh?

Musical Number 4: The Land and Honey (reprise)

And now that Bob La Follette went
and swept the bosses out,
the air is clean, and so is ... the government:
our dear Wisconsin ... democracy.

Mary: We couldn't think of anything to rhyme with "out"!

19

Phil: Except "trout". We have those in Wisconsin!

Bob: Or sauerkraut!

Phil: We'll have to keep working on it.

[Everyone laughs. Bobbie, Phil and Mary run, followed by Fola, to hug Belle. Belle kisses Bob.]

Belle: What did we do to deserve this?

Bob: We must have angered the muse of poetry somewhere along the way.

[Fola moves forward. Lights/curtain down.]

Fola: In case I forgot to mention it, both Mom and Dad were born and raised in Wisconsin. They grew up with the state, and they loved it. Bob was born in 1855, when the state itself was only seven years old. By the time he was ten, he'd seen the effects of war, the Civil War, not first hand, but through those who returned, and those who didn't return. His father died, too, of natural causes, when Bob was only a year old, and a stepfather died when Bob was sixteen, leaving him as the responsible man on the family farm, and he shouldered responsibility well. Nevertheless, as he was growing up, he also managed to be a boy, and like all boys, he occasionally got into trouble. One day Bob and some of his friends managed to separate a large ice floe on the Pecatonica River and rode it several miles downstream before they could find a way to get off. And then there was the time ...

Scene 3: The Blue Savage

Instrumental music which continues as various
children perform. Bob's lines are
spoken over it.

[Fola exits. Lights/curtain up to show various children
performing circus acts as other (especially younger) children
watch. This can go on for some time. Any number of
children's lines can be interpolated. Bob can be given lines
to introduce or comment on the various acts.]

Child: Show us the wild man, Bob. I want to see the wild
man.

Bob: Step right up. Come one, come all. See the eighth
wonder of the world right here in Primrose. One day only.
Tell your friends. It's a genuine wild man, brought here at
great expense from Borneo. The price is only a nickel, one-
twentieth of a dollar; if you need change, just holler. And
now, straight from Borneo, behold!

[Curtains are withdrawn revealing a "cage" containing a boy
painted blue. The boy acts the savage, then escapes from his
"cage" and runs wild, causing pandemonium among the
younger children. Bob's mother enters.]

Mary: Robert Marion LaFollette, what are you doing?!

Bob: Nothing, Mom.

Mary: Josephine, did you let your brother do this?

Josephine: Mom, you know I can't stop Bob from doing

21

anything he sets his mind to.

Mary: Who is this?

Bob: That's just Lars.

Mary: Well, that's enough. You all go home now. Not you, Lars. We'll have to see what we can do to remove some of this indigo before you go home.

Lars: If I'm gonna have t' get scrubbed, I'd jus' as soon do that at home, if you don' mind, Missus La Follette.

Mary: All right, I suppose so. Go on then. But you make sure you tell your mother that I didn't know anything about this.

Lars: This isn't gonna get Bob into trouble, is it? I mean, it wasn't just his idea, and ever'body had a lot o' fun until ...

Mary: Until I came along? No, Bob isn't in trouble, but we'll have a little talk.

[Lars looks at Bob.]

Bob: It's all right. I'll see you at school tomorrow.

Lars: You bet. 'Bye.

Bob: 'Bye.

Mary: Good-bye, Lars. Oh Bob, you're such a wild boy.

Bob: Mom, nobody got hurt. Even the little kids were having fun.

Mary: Maybe, but you don't realize what the sound of children screaming in terror does to a mother.

Bob: Sorry, Mom, but if I'd told you what we were doing, you prob'ly wouldn't've let us do it.

Mary: Josephine --

Josephine: Mom, really. Nobody got hurt. It just sounded like --

Mary: Like bedlam, like every child in Primrose was being chased by a mad dog.

Josephine: Mom --

Mary: It's all right. I'm feeling calmer now. Oh Bob, what will I do for excitement when you're gone.

Bob: I'm not going anywhere.

Mary: No, you're such a smart boy. When the time comes, I want you to go to college, even if we have to sell part of the farm to do it.

Bob: But the farm was Dad's.

Mary: The farm's important, but you know what your father left that's even more important than the farm?

[Bob thinks for awhile.]

Bob: No, what.

Mary: You. He left us you. You have to make the most of your life, for him, and for yourself. When you grow up, you can be anything you choose to be, even president of the United States.

Bob: No thanks, I think I'll be a farmer, or maybe a carnival barker. Neither of you went to college.

Mary: There was no college. Your father and I made a good life, but the country's changing. Education's more important now. This was a frontier prairie when we moved here. Now it's settled, civilized. Men like your father, and you, look at the world, see its opportunities and seize them, see its problems and work to solve them. He was town clerk, and he was elected town chairman the year you were born.

Bob: I know, Mom. He was town clerk, and he was elected town chairman the year I was born.

[Mary shows a moment of anger; she may even move to strike him.]

Mary: I don't ever want to hear you show disrespect to your father. He'd want you to grow up and make something of yourself. If he were still alive, I'm sure he'd be leading the movement to regulate the railroads. The issues may be different when you grow up, but you'll know how to face them.

Bob: That's a tall order, Mom.

Mary: I have great faith in you, Son. Just remember who you are, where you come from, and where you stand.

<u>Musical number 6: Horizons on the Prairie</u>

Horizons on the prairie have no end,
and every road's beginning can be here.
Some day you'll choose a path and follow it;

The winds may buffet you, the storm may rise,
There may be times when you are by yourself.

Remember when you find yourself alone
or find you're in a strange and lonely place
that your beginning always will be here,
the tall pines and the wild places.

Home is where the heart revives,
it never disappears;
your dreams may carry you away,
but home is always here.

Hold fast to your memories:
the eagle's flight above,
the tall pines and the fertile fields
and most, your parents' love.

Home is where the heart revives,
it never disappears;
your dreams may carry you away,
but home is always here.

Bob: [to Josephine] I'll civilize you.

[He chases her off. Fola enters from the wing.
Lights/curtain down.]

Fola: Civilized, indeed. Bob eventually did become

25

civilized, but only with a little assistance from my mother. They met when they were both students at the University of Wisconsin from 1875 to 1879. They shared an appreciation of learning, of language, and of each other.

[Fola exits. Lights/curtain up.]

Scene 4: College and Belle

[Bob is working in the office of the University Press. Students 1 and 2 come on or poke their heads in.]

Student 1: Hey Bob, congratulations on that speech. You really had the audience in the palm of your hand.

Student 2: Yeah, you're just a natural-born speaker. You could've heard a pin drop in there, if you hadn't been talking, I mean. Aw, you know what I mean.

Bob: Thanks.

Student 1: Hey, we're going to the Granger rally, protest the railroad monopolies. Do you want to come with us?

Bob: I can't. I have to get this edition of "The Press" out by deadline. I've got Tom Hintleman going to the rally to report on it.

Student 1: Oh come on. Ever since you bought this paper, you've been too busy to have fun.

Student 2: Yeah. We could always count on you to lead the fun or come up with a new prank. What happened to you, anyway.

Bob: I've got my mother and sister to take care of. You two go on. I'll try to catch up with you later.

Student 2: Have it your way. If you don't show up, we'll stop by on our way back to see if you can break away.

Bob: You bet. And if I'm far enough along, I'll go with

you.

[The students leave.]

Bob: Choices.

Musical Number 7: How Do I Choose?

How do I choose.
How do I know what I choose'll be right.

I can go wherever I want to go.
I can be whatever I want to be.

How do I choose who I'm to be, and
How do I know what I choose'll be right.

I can dream old dreams I have dreamed before,
I can dream new dreams, let my fancy soar.

How do I choose.
How do I know what I choose'll be right.

I know how to farm, I know how to write,
I can shave and trim, I can set up type.

How do I choose.
How do I know what I choose'll be right.

The horizon calls, and I must not stay;
It will soon be time to elect my way.

How do I choose.
How do I know what I choose'll be right.

28

How do I choose.
How do I know what I choose'll be right.

I can go wherever I want to go.
I can be whatever I want to be.

How do I choose who I'm to be, and
How do I know what I choose'll be right.

[Belle enters.]

Belle: Bob, hello.

Bob: Belle! I was hoping you'd stop by.

Belle: I just had to, to tell you how wonderful your oration was. Everyone was mesmerized.

Bob: Yours was great, too!

Belle: Oh no, I was terrified. Thanks again for helping me. I'll never be as good as you.

Bob: But in every other subject, you're way out ahead of me. You get A's and I ... don't.

Belle: That's because you're involved in so many other things.

Bob: Besides, you do better than you think at oration. Here, look at this.

Belle: You reprinted my whole speech.

Bob: "If a girl spends the best part of her childhood playing with [an inanimate] doll, she will spend the best part of her girlhood in dreaming dreams of impossible future happiness, [and] she will spend the best part of her womanhood in learning how unreal were the dreams of her girlhood." Belle, that's wonderful. People who weren't there should read what you said. Here, see what I wrote.

Belle: "For force and originality of thought, it was not equaled during the evening." Am I blushing? It wasn't that good, even with your help. But where's the coverage of your speech.

Bob: I thought it would be too much. Listen, Belle, you've been my closest friend since freshman year.

Belle: Ever since you organized the students to stand up for [Rachel]when she was almost expelled.

Bob: Aw, that was nothing.

Belle: I've never forgotten it. You're a natural leader.

Bob: You know, there's something I've been wanting to tell you for a long time. I never told you about this, but in the middle of sophomore year, the dean wanted to expel you, too.

Belle: What?! He .... No. I never did anyth --

Bob: Never did anything bad in your life, is that what you mean? Oh, you'd be surprised what I know and what the dean knows, about you.

Belle: You are kidding me, aren't you?

Bob: Course I am. And it's probably true that you never did anything bad in your whole life. Except maybe last Saturday night.

Belle: Shh.

Bob: If I apologize for kidding you, can I have a kiss?

Belle: Even without the apology.

[They kiss.]

Bob: Belle ....

Belle: Yes?

Bob: I ... [Beat.] I'm working on a new oration.

Belle: You are? What's the topic, or can you tell me.

Bob: Only you. It's another one from the theater. The villain from Othello.

Belle: Iago?

Bob: Yes. I already know some of what I'm going to say. What do you think of this: "Iago lacks the most vital attribute of life, a developed moral sense." "He is skeptical of all virtue, and to him love is lechery, truth-telling is stupid goodness, and lying is a daring to be ingenious."

Belle: Good language, good insight. You don't feel that way about love, do you?

Bob: Of course not! That's why he's such a villain. Do

31

you?

Belle: Not at all. [Beat] What are you preparing it for.

Bob: The state contest in Beloit [pronounced buh-LOYT].

Belle: Oh Bob, I know you'll win. There's no-one who can come within a hundred miles of your oratorical skills.

Bob: Thanks. Knowing that you have such confidence in me helps a lot.

Belle: And what if you do ... win.

Bob: Then there's the inter-state championship in Iowa City.

Belle: That'll be exciting. I'll come and watch you win that, too.

Bob: You bet.

Belle: And then a national contest in Washington, judged by President Hayes himself?

Bob: No, afraid not. You'll never catch me trying to win a national contest. But, you know, I've been giving quite a bit of thought to what I'll do after I graduate. That is, if I graduate. My grades aren't nearly as good as yours.

Belle: You'll graduate. I'll help you. We'll work together, just as we always have. Will you continue to publish the paper?

Bob: I could. This has been a good investment. It helped support me and my mom and my sister, but it doesn't make enough money for ...

Belle: Are you still thinking of being an actor?

Bob: What a question, right after I said publishing a paper doesn't make enough money! No, [I think of it all the time, but I guess Mr. McCullough was right. I'm too short to be either a convincing hero or a threatening villain. I'd be relegated to minor roles.] I considered going back to barbering, but I didn't really like it. What I've been thinking about is going to law school.

Belle: Really? Yes, you could be a good lawyer, but ... your grades?

Bob: I know, but I think I could do it, if I really work at it. And maybe if you'll continue to help me.

Belle: Well, I don't know --

Bob: If I were a lawyer, I could make enough money to take care of myself and Mom and Josephine ... and you.

Belle: Me!? What are you talking about! You don't need to worry about that. I'm planning to take care of myself. What in the world --

[A student pokes his/her head in the door.]

Student 2: Hey Bob. Are you sure you can't join us? Come see who's here.

Bob: Uh, sure. Belle, could you excuse me? I'll be right back.

[Bob leaves with the student.]

Belle: Of course. What did he mean by that. He isn't serious. Could he have been joking? That didn't sound like one of his jokes. And he wouldn't tease me like that ... about that. [Pause.] But am I ready for that? No. Not now. I have to finish school. We both have to. But even after graduation ... There's so much I want to do. [Beat.] What do I want. What do I expect.

<u>Musical Number 8: Who Tells Me What I Should Be?</u>

Here at the dawn of my day
in the epoch of womanhood's birth,
I seek my particular way
to honor my place on the earth.

I know I have talents to use
in the public arena of life.
Would I sacrifice all, would I lose,
if I turned into somebody's wife?

Who tells me what I should be,
what I should say, where I should go.
Who shows me what path to take,
is it with him, or is it for me.

What shall I say to him now?
Would I cease being true to myself?
If I should accede to that vow,
Would I put all my dreams on the shelf?

Soon I must say yes or no.
Should I give away hand, heart and head?

34

I love him, but how can I know
what my life will become if I wed.

Who tells me what I should be,
what I should say, where I should go.
Who shows me what path to take,
is it with him, or is it for me.

And yet should I fail to embrace
the joys of a family, too.
I'll miss out on love and romance.
Oh, how shall I know just what to do.

Who tells me what I should be,
what I should say, where I should go.
Who shows me what path to take,
is it with him, or is it for me.

Who knows what to do ...
[Bob returns.]

Bob: Belle.

Belle: Yes?

Bob: I'm back.

Belle: I see.

Bob: I told them I had more important things to take care of.

Belle: Yes, that's what you said just before you left.

Bob: I did?

Belle: You said you had to take care of yourself and your family and all of your closest friends.

Bob: It wasn't all of my friends. It was just you.

Belle: I was afraid of that.

Bob: Afraid?

Belle: Because you're getting very serious.

Bob: I am. You may have laughed when I said it, but I was serious. I'm asking if you'd marry me.

Belle: We've been such great friends. Do you think we could be ... more than that?

Bob: I'm certain of it.

Belle: But you do mean after we graduate, don't you?

Bob: Of course.

Belle: And how would we live, especially if you decide to study law. I was planning to teach school, but we can hardly live on that.

Bob: We can put off getting married for awhile. I don't have it all figured out yet. I had to start by asking you. But if you say "yes", then we can try to figure it out together. I know I can do anything I put my mind to.

Belle: Yes, you can, including getting me to say yes, if you're truly serious.

Bob: I'm not joking.

Belle: Then ... I seriously agree.

Bob: You do?

Belle: I do.

[He starts to kiss her.]

Belle: I have one request, that you might find strange.

Bob: What's that.

Belle: When people get married, the woman vows to "love, honor and obey". Do you think we could go with just the first two?

Bob: I do.

Belle: Thank you.

<u>Musical Number 9: How Do I Choose? & Who Tells Me What I Should Be?</u> (reprise)

(Belle) Now, now that my choice is clear:
I want myself, and us.
Now, if we can live as peers,
I'll give to you all of my love.
We'll know what to do.
I do.

(Bob) Now I choose;
now I know what I choose'll be right.
We'll be together;

building a future our dreams we'll unite.
I'll be with you, and you'll be with me.
We'll know what to do.
I do.

[They kiss. Fola comes out. Curtain/lights down.]

Fola: Belle was also from a small town in Wisconsin. She grew up in Baraboo. Although she was four years younger than Bob, they were in the same class at the University. She was a spirited young woman, especially for the times.

Bob completed his study of law quickly and by 1880, he decided to run for his first elective office, Dane County District Attorney. That campaign set the mold for the pattern he followed during the rest of his life, of independence within the political party system. The Republican Party had been born in a schoolhouse in Ripon, Wisconsin, in 1854, and Bob's uncles were among its first members. Bob became a Republican and although he continually pushed the party in new and uncomfortable directions, he always considered himself a Republican. When he decided to run for Dane County D.A., he approached a person known as "Boss Keyes", the most powerful man in the local Republican party. Boss Keyes informed Bob that he had someone else in mind for that position, but my father didn't accept that. He borrowed a buggy, hitched his horse to it, and personally visited every voter in Dane County that he could reach. Since it was harvest time, he made his rounds to the farmers in the evenings, and his opponents began referring to him as a "night rider". As my mother said later, he went to work "as though his life depended on winning the office". When the dust settled, Robert La Follette was D.A., and "Fighting Bob" had been born.

38

As District Attorney, he had a steady job with a modest but steady income. A little over a year later, he and Belle married.

Scene 5: La Follette and La Follette

[Bob and the attorney enter the Dane County District Attorney's office.]

Attorney: You know, you just can't send my client to jail. He really didn't ...

Bob: I'm sorry, Walter, but the sheriff just had to talk to me for a minute. You know how it is.

Attorney: Yeah. Clients! You can't live with'm and you can't live without'm. What was it this time, another petty theft?

Bob: How did you know?

Attorney: It was all over the courthouse this morning. That'll be a more difficult case than you expect.

Bob: Just because it involves a politician?

Attorney: You don't think that makes a --

[Belle knocks.]

Bob: Yes?

Belle: Are you busy?

Bob: Just for another minute or two. Can you wait?

Belle: Of course.

Bob: Now what were you saying out in the hall, that your

40

client didn't do it?

Attorney: Of course not.

Bob: I have a witness who says he did.

Attorney: Patrick Fernan? [This name should be changed nightly, to the name of a local figure, preferably one in the audience.] Forgive me for saying this, but nobody in his right mind would build a case on that disreputable old drunkard. Besides, I've got two witnesses who'll tell you my client was nowhere near the tavern that night.

Bob: If you want to tell me who your witnesses are and what they have to say, and I find them believeable, I'll re-consider the charge.

Attorney: It's a deal. I'll get you written statements by next week.

Bob: All right. We'll talk about it again then.

Attorney: Thanks. That's all I ask. I'll see you around.

Bob: Next week.

[The attorney opens the door and leaves.]

Attorney: Mrs. La Follette.

Belle: Hello, Walter.

[Belle enters, carrying a small basket or briefcase.]

Bob: Mrs. La Follette. [He kisses her, not passionately, but

41

not perfunctorily; after all, they're newly wed.] What a pleasant surprise, but what are you doing here.

Belle: The only way I get to see you these days is to come here.

Bob: Now Belle ...

Belle: If you hadn't made that campaign promise to prosecute all the cases personally to save money, you might come home on evenings or weekends.

Bob: And if I hadn't made that campaign promise, I might not have been elected; and if I hadn't kept that campaign promise in my first term, I almost certainly wouldn't have been re-elected. You've got to appeal directly to the voters and be honest with them.

Belle: I know. I expect no less from you.

Bob: I've got to work hard if I want to run for Congress.

Belle: That's why I decided to leave Fola with Mary next door for awhile and bring you a healthy supper.

Bob: That was swell of you. Did you bring me something else?

Belle: Why yes, how did you know.

Bob: Just let me lock the door for a little while.

[He goes to the door and locks it.]

Belle: Oh, now wait. Not that I don't think that's a

wonderful idea. But first, I really did bring you something else.

Bob: Nothing that important, I'm sure.

Belle: Just the brief for the Willet case.

Bob: You finished it already?

Belle: I told you I would. It was fascinating. I think you'll enjoy seeing how I used Blackstone.

Bob: You're wonderful. That reminds me. We got a major compliment today.

Belle: Oh? From whom.

Bob: Justice Lyon. He told me "my" brief in the Baker case was one of the best briefs submitted to the court in years.

Belle: Oh Bob!

Bob: I was pleased to tell him that you wrote it.

Belle: You didn't.

Bob: Why shouldn't I.

Belle: Well, ...

Bob: And he said you should become a lawyer.

Belle: Did you tell him?

Bob: That you'll be the first woman law school graduate in

Wisconsin? Nope, I didn't think it was that important.

Belle: What?

Bob: Yes, I told him. I'm so proud of you.

Belle: And what was his reaction. No jokes, please.

Bob: He was all for it. He thought La Follette and La Follette would be a very successful firm.

Belle: Partners?

Bob: We already are, aren't we?

<u>Musical Number 10: Partners</u>

Partners,
in work and play.
Partners,
both night and day.
Partners,
that's how we'll be successful.

Partners,
through thick and thin.
Partners,
we both will win.
Partners,
regardless of our critics.

No path we take is certain,
we'll question what to do.
Whatever happens happens,
'cause I'll be right here with you.

44

Partners,
we'll share our lot.
Partners,
whate'er we've got.
Partners,
it's mutual assistance.

Partners,
we're mister and madame.
Partners,
like Eve and Adam.
Partners,
we share and share alike.

No path we take is certain,
we'll question what to do.
Whatever happens happens,
'cause I'll be right here with you.

We -- you mean me? --
you and I, we'll always be around
to help -- Watch out! -- Oh my! --
each other out.

The older generation won't know what our team's
        about.
When you're in trouble, all you have to do is shout.
Hey you, come over here.

Partners,
in work and play.
Partners,
both night and day.
Partners,

that's how we'll be successful.

Partners,
that's how we'll be successful.
Partners,
that's how we'll be successful.

Partners?
Partners.

[Bob and Belle embrace. Lights/curtain down. Fola enters from the wing.]

Fola: Bob worked hard to win elections and, once elected, he worked hard to live up to the people's trust. In 1884, he was elected to the U.S. Congress, and he established a reputation for honesty, integrity and courage. One incident in particular crystallized that reputation.

[Fola exits. Well-dressed couples begin to enter. Lights/curtain up.]

Scene 6: Politics and Money

[An elegant ballroom in the Plankinton Hotel in Milwaukee.
Some of the couples dance while others watch and
converse.]

Musical Number 11: The Lobbyists' Waltz

We help senators,
assemblymen, too,
decide how to vote,
decide what to do.

We give them the facts
they need to take stands:
to let railroads thrive,
to log public lands.

It's the lobbyists' waltz, the lobbyists' waltz,
a dance very simple to learn.
The steps are not hard, they're really not hard:
we curtsey, we bow, and then turn, again and again.

When facts aren't enough,
and someone needs cash,
we contribute a bit:
largesse with panache.

The reps are out front
where everyone sees.
We work in the shadows,
l'eminence grise.

We turn again and again.

It's the lobbyists' waltz, the lobbyists' waltz,
a dance very simple to learn.
The steps are not hard, they're really not hard:
we curtsey, we bow, and then turn, again and again.

And then turn, and then turn, and then turn, and then
        turn,
and then end The Lobbyists' Waltz.

[Senator Sawyer enters. Politicians and lobbyists gather
around him.]

Musical Number 12: Monopolies Grow and Profits Flow

Railroad lines and lumber yards,
packing houses, private guards.
Monopolies grow and profits flow;
we're the ones with all the cards.

Nothing matches quite the thrill
of plunging hands deep in the till.
We set the rates, and emulate
J. P. Morgan and James Hill.

America, land of the free,
unbridled opportunity.
Free to earn obscene returns.
The rich enjoy prosperity.

Advice to workers who must toil,
and farmers grubbing in the soil:
just up and buy a world's supply,
like Rockefeller's Standard Oil.

America, land of the free,
unbridled opportunity.
Free to earn obscene returns.
The rich enjoy prosperity.

Money money money money,
folks without it, we all shun.
Equality? Now don't be funny.
That's what makes Wisconsin sunny.

America, land of the free.

[Bob enters.]

Sawyer: Here he comes, boys. Leave me to talk to him alone. Congressman La Follette.

Bob: Senator Sawyer.

Sawyer: Thank you for coming up to Milwaukee to see me.

Bob: It's my pleasure, but why all the mystery about this meeting. Why invite me here using unmarked stationery and then ask me to telegraph you back with just "yes" or "no".

Sawyer: Oh that's just my way. I like t' add a little spice t' ev'rything I do. You know, you're a real credit to our Republican delegation in Washington.

Bob: Why thank you. I'm a little surprised to hear you say that.

Sawyer: Just because you bucked boss Keyes and ran without his blessing?

Bob: Well, yes.

Sawyer: Hey, I may be a politician, but I'm also a businessman. I've learned that you don't argue with success. That just shows that you know how to take the main chance. And hell, you're still Republican.

Bob: And proud of it.

Sawyer: Good, because I, I need to appeal to you as a fellow Republican.

Bob: Oh?

Sawyer: Your brother-in-law is a judge now.

Bob: You didn't call me here to congratulate me on that.

Sawyer: Since you're no longer D.A., maybe you don't keep up on the local cases much any more, but he was assigned a mighty important case, against the Republican state treasurer.

Bob: Harshaw. I know.

Sawyer: Oh, have you talked to him about it?

Bob: A little.

Sawyer: That's good.

Bob: Why.

Sawyer: Then you could talk to him some more.

Bob: What do you mean.

Sawyer: A fellow Republican's in trouble. Harshaw didn't take that money, and even if he did, it wasn't enough to make such a fuss about. I'd like you to help out.

Bob: How.

Sawyer: Well, I'd like you to explain to Judge Siebecker, some night over dinner ...

Bob: You want me to try to influence that case?

Sawyer: Oh don't worry. I'm not asking you to do it for charity, even if it is for a fellow party member.

[Sawyer holds out a roll of bills.]

Bob: What's that!

Sawyer: Let's just call it a retainer, for your law firm to do some work on the case.

Bob: You're offering me a bribe!

Sawyer: No, we don't call it that.

Bob: No lawyer -- no honest lawyer -- gets a retainer that big handed to him, in cash, before the terms are even arranged. If this is the way you do your business, you'll find you've made a huge mistake!

Sawyer: You misunderstand me.

Bob: I don't think so. You misjudge me. You and I may be in the same party, but we are not kindred. Good-bye!

Sawyer: Wait!

Musical Number 13: The Game

(Recitative) You think that you're above this all.
Well, let me set you straight.

You claim to be an honest pol;
I've not seen one to date.

I can't tell if you're just naive
or seek to make a name,

But either way you'll soon find out
you've got to play the game.

(Song) We're in this game together.
We help each other out.
No-one survives on principle.
Of that there is no doubt.

I'm merely asking you to help
a fellow Republican,
a treasurer who's been accused
of taking what he can.

You scratch my back and I'll scratch yours.
You guard my back and I'll guard yours.
It's mutual, my friend; it's mutual.
And then you're learning how to play The Game.

You bucked the local boss to win
election as D.A.,

but now that you're a congressman,
you'll have to learn to play.

The voter doesn't matter;
just write that sucker off.
The ones that has are all you need
to keep you at the trough.

You scratch my back and I'll scratch yours.
You guard my back and I'll guard yours.
It's mutual, my friend; it's mutual.
And then you're learning how to play The Game.

Bob: [speaking during musical break] What if I turn it down
and walk away. Will I be unemployed in two more years?
Will I be ostracized, hung out to dry? Or is my honesty
worth hanging for.

(Bob) I can't believe, I won't accept
the course that you advise.
Are politicians all corrupt
and honesty despised?

(lobbyist or politician) Who said a thing about
            corruption?
We just work together.
Members of a club are we,
political birds of a feather.

You scratch my back and I'll scratch yours.
You guard my back and I'll guard yours.
It's mutual, my friend; it's mutual.
And then you're learning how to play ...

Bob: No! Good-bye!

[Bob slams a door and exits.]

(chorus) The Game.

[Lights/curtain down. End of Act 1.]

ACT 2

Scene 7: The Governor's Holiday Ball - Part 2

[Bob, Belle, Fola, Bobbie, Phil, and Mary start in the same position they were in at the end of scene 2.]

Belle: What did we do to derserve this?

Bob: We must have angered the muse of poetry somewhere along the way.

Phil: I see a carriage. Someone's coming.

[Guests arrive. There are greetings, taking of coats, mingling and conversation. A man and a woman, obviously a couple, approach Bob.]

Man 1: Governor, I voted for you every time you ran for anything, ever since your first race for District Attorney. You visited my farm --

Bob: Wait. Don't tell me. Nils Larson. And your farm is west of Roxbury on the river.

Man 1: Right, by god.

Bob: Hvordan står det til.

Man 1: Bare bra. Oh, excuse me. Governor La Follette, this is my wife, Kirsten Larson.

Bob: I'm pleased to meet you.

Woman 1: The pleasure's mine. I'm a schoolteacher, as

your wife was, and I can't tell you how good it's made me feel to have someone who values education, first in the governor's mansion and now going to represent us in Washington.

Bob: Thank you, Missus Larson.

Woman 1: If women only had the vote, you'd have mine. To have the whole country describe a partnership between the government and the university as "the Wisconsin idea" just makes me proud.

Bob: And it works. It's good to meet you, and to see you again. Enjoy yourself.

John Ringling: Do you remember me, Miss Case?

Belle: Miss Case? Were you one of my students?

John Ringling: I admit I never had much affinity for book-learnin', but I alway remember your class fondly. Step right up, ladies and gentlemen, to see the Greatest Show on Earth!

Belle: John Ringling! I've followed your career with great interest and pride. I used to criticize you for paying more attention to those children's circuses and sideshows you put on than to your studies. It just shows how wrong a person -- even a well-intentioned teacher -- can be. You've managed to put Baraboo back on the map, after that Count with the unpronounceable name took all his grapes and went to California, and after our hop capitol of the world was laid low by a little louse.

Bob: Are you talking about me?

Belle: No, I'm afraid you haven't had that much influence on the state's economy. I have the pleasure of presenting John Ringling. Mr. Ringling, my husband the governor.

John Ringling: I'm pleased to meet you.

Bob: I'm delighted to make your acquaintance. My wife keeps telling me that your name and your achievements will be remembered long after I'm gone and forgotten in this state.

Man 2: I seen ya over t' Muscoda [pronounced MUS-cuh-day], standin' on the farm wagon. Ya ain't so tall in person. Man, you was talkin' up a storm. The only thing I remember is that story you told about Governor Scofield's cow and how it got a pass from a railroad lobbyist t' ride free. That got me t' vote fer ya.

Bob: I hope Governor Scofield's cow is enjoying its retirement from public life.

Belle: Zona! Welcome to our holiday party. I'm so glad you could come tonight.

Zona Gale: I'm so glad to be here, and to see your whole family again. I'll be sorry when you leave this state, but I sure wish I could see their faces in Washington when they find out what kind of man we're sending there as Senator and what our Wisconsin Progressive movement is. You know what they're saying in Milwaukee: "Take it from John Jacob Astor, La Follette will be a disaster," but the question is "for whom?" Where are your children.

Belle: Over there. Let me introduce them to you.

Man 3 or Woman: I can't wait until you impose Robert's Rules of Order on the Senate.

John Bascom: Master La Follette.

Bob: President Bascom! What an unexpected pleasure. I'm delighted to see you again, and to thank you again. I certainly wouldn't be here today --

John Bascom: If I hadn't cast the deciding vote to let you graduate. How well I know. The faculty was sharply divided over your grades.

Bob: How well I know.

John Bascom: But grades aren't everything. I didn't think any man could take on the railroads and win, but you did. I salute you.

Bob: Thank you. I've always treasured your faith in me.

John Bascom: And I see your wife, the good student, over there. I must say hello to her, too.

Bob: Well, friends, I don't want to make a speech --

Belle: That will be a first.

Bob: but since I'll be bidding good-bye to this office soon, and my responsibilities to the people of this state will be changing, I just want to say that "If it can be shown that Wisconsin is a happier and better state to live in, that its institutions are more democratic, that the opportunities of all its people are more equal, that social justice more nearly prevails, that human life is safer and sweeter -- then I shall

rest content in the feeling that the Progressive movement and
I have been successful." Now I invite you all to enjoy the
refreshments, and dance a little. After all, this is a ball.
Musicians, a polka.

Musical Number 14: Party Dance.

[People start getting coats, saying "Good-bye", etc. Bob,
Belle and the children start singing and everyone picks it up
as they leave. On the repeat of the last verse, Bob, Belle and
the children exit.]

Musical Number 15: Christmas Spirit

Bells are ringing, children singing,
Carols and songs of good cheer.
Snow is falling, friends are calling in this
wonderful time of year.

Cold November, bleak December,
season of threatening night.
We foresee the heav'nly light
that puts winter's darkness to flight.

Bells are ringing, children singing,
Carols and songs of good cheer.
Snow is falling, friends are calling in this
wonderful time of the year.

Christmas spirit, now you hear it
rising again and again.
Never cease, that sweet song of peace,
on earth good will to all men.

Bells are ringing, children singing,

Carols and songs of good cheer.
Snow is falling, friends are calling in this
wonderful time of the year.

That wonderful time of year.

[Fola comes forward. Lights/curtain down behind her.]

Fola: Mom and Dad came to be well-loved during the six
years he served as governor. Of course, he made enemies,
too, especially among the business interests which tried to
feather their own nests at the expense of the common people.
It was while he was governor that I began my career in the
theater. As I mentioned, I was much older than Bobbie, Phil
and Mary, and it wasn't long before I was on the stage in
New York City, and I became a founding member of Actors
Equity. I met and married George Middleton, a playwright
and himself a founding member of the Dramatists Guild.

In 1905, my father was elected to the U.S. Senate, and he
served as senator from Wisconsin for almost twenty years.
His convictions endured their greatest test in 1917. He was
in the U.S. Senate then, and he and a handful of other
Senators opposed U.S. entry into the European War, the one
that came to be known as World War I. Since then, it's
become pretty patriotic to support our country in war,
especially the Second World War, but you know, we still
sent fifty thousand American men to their graves -- not to try
to even count the hundreds of thousands from other countries
who died -- and a lot of people agree that the second great
war wouldn't have happened if there'd been a just peace
after the first one. That treaty, the Treaty of Versailles, was
another battle my father fought and lost; he considered it to
be one of the worst agreements ever made. He stood almost
alone in those fights.

[Fola exits. Lights/curtain up. The three senators walk on.]

Scene 8: Mr. La Follette Goes to Washington

<u>Musical Number 16: War.</u>

No-one wants to go to war --
we all know war is hell --
but if we were to go to war,
we might do very well.

No-one wants to go to war --
we say that with true zeal --
but if we were to go to war,
the war'd be good for steel.

We'd never vote for anything that wasn't good for
      all,
for if we did, we might become a target for recall.

No-one wants to go to war --
that feeling's genuine --
but if we were to go to war,
the profits would roll in.

No-one wants to go to war --
we three the least of all --
but if we were to go to war,
we'd help them heed the call.

We'd never vote for anything that wasn't good for
      all,
for if we did, we might become a target for recall.
War!

61

Bob: This is a war among the imperial and colonial powers of Europe. American interests are remote and insignificant compared to the economic disaster wrought by war. War is the money-changer's opportunity and the social reformer's doom. It is an investment for the rich, to be re-paid by taxing all, including those who can least afford it. The poor are the ones who will be called upon to rot in the trenches, but the poor have no organized voice to speak out against war. The rich have many voices here. My fellow senators, I have here the results of a referendum on the war question in Monroe, Wisconsin. For peace, 954, for war, 95. The message --

Senator 1: Will the speaker yield?

Bob: No!

Senator 1: But the senator has been speaking for eight hours.

Bob: And I plan to go on for another eight. "I will continue on this floor until I complete my statement unless someone carries me off, and I should like to see the man who will try it."

[Senator 1 stands, puts his hand in his pocket, and takes a step toward Bob. Senator Lane stands, puts his hand in his pocket, and moves toward him.]

Senator Lane: We all know you carry a revolver. Do you really plan to use it here on the floor? Come on then.

[Senator 1 looks at Senator Lane and at Bob, then turns around and leaves. Senator Lane follows him out. Other

62

senators get up and start to leave.]

Senator 2: But if we don't take action on this bill before we adjourn at noon tomorrow, the President won't be able to arm American ships.

Bob: Which means we just might stay out of this war. I will note for the record that certain Senators are leaving the chamber. They may not be interested in what I have to say, but the public is interested.

Senator 2: Is the senator aware that he is being hanged and burned in effigy around the country for his obstinate and obstructionist position on this issue.

Bob: I certainly am aware, but do you really think that would cause me to change my convictions? How much less the danger from being burned in effigy than from being shot right here in this chamber. I have been counseled by more sensible voices than yours to have more regard for my personal safety than for my convictions. I can only say that "Fear and worry are futile, and wasted energy which should be conserved for the work at hand."

Senator 3: Is the senator aware that he has been publicly condemned by a majority of faculty members at his own alma mater, the University of Wisconsin?

Bob: I am, and it saddens me. Nevertheless, do you think that would cause me to change my convictions?

Senator 3: Yes, by god. Why not.

Bob: Because that vote followed a series of attacks on the University by the "Loyalty Legions" for its not being patriotic enough, and I realize that even the protective walls of academe cannot halt the spread of hysteria or the fear of being labeled "unpatriotic".

Senator 3: Is the senator aware that President Wilson himself is in direct opposition to your stand, that he has released a statement condemning the "little group of willful men, representing no opinion but their own, [who] have rendered the great government of the United States helpless and contemptible"?

Bob: I take heart from that statement, not because I would ever want to render our government contemptible, but because I do desire to render our government incapable of thoughtlessly and foolishly being swept along by war fever into a European conflict in which thousands, perhaps tens of thousands of Americans would die needlessly. I will continue to do all in my power to achieve that end.

Senator 3: You refuse to support the President in the country's hour of need?

Bob: I shall support the President in the measures he proposes when I believe them to be right. I shall oppose measures proposed by the President when I believe them to be wrong.

[Senator 2 and 3 leave. Bob and the President of the Senate are alone.]

President of the Senate: Mr. La Follette, since you seem to be alone on the floor, I will declare a fifteen-minute recess for the convenience and comfort of those of us who are left. You may continue speaking when we reconvene.

[The President of the Senate leaves.]

Bob: Solé e desolé. Alone and desolate. Tired, too.
[spoken over chords in the orchestra] What
difference does it make if I am right
when everyone condemns my stand as wrong? How
difficult it is to stay the course, how easy it would
be to just give in.
[recitative] Who am I to stop the thunderstorm?
Who am I to calm the sea's dark swell? Why stand
alone upon the threatened shore? Why raise my
voice to drown the ocean's roar?

Musical Number 17: I Stand Alone
I stand alone, none by my side.
My strength, exhausted, fails.

[Bobbie enters.]

Bobbie: Dad?

Bob: Bobbie, what are you doing here. Is everything all
right in the office?

Bobbie: The office is fine. Is everything all right here?

Bob: I'm feeling a little low. Not defeated, just ... tired.

Bobbie: I brought you a telegram.

Bob: Do you have any idea how many telegrams we've
received in the past two days alone?

Bobbie: I certainly do. I've opened them all myself.

Bob: Then why deliver this one.

Bobbie: Well, ... it's from Mom.

Bob: Is she all right?!

Bobbie: Oh yeah. I just thought you'd like to read it right away.

Bob: Missus Belle La Follette, Maple Bluff Farm, Madison, Wisconsin.

[A light comes up to reveal Belle on a portion of the stage.]

Belle: Dearest Bob, I am so sorry that my Chatauqua schedule and the magazine deadline prevent me from being present in the gallery watching you today as on so many other occasions, but I am with you in spirit. I follow every hour's report of your battle in the Senate, and not a minute passes when I don't think of you, imagining just how you are standing and just what you are saying. I worry about your health, as I always do, but I know you will do what is right, regardless. "It is my heartfelt conviction that you are rendering the world the greatest service it has ever come to you to render and that you are using the power and opportunity that is yours for humanity and democracy. I cannot see how you could take any other course and I am filled with a deep sense of thanksgiving beyond all words to express."

<u>Musical Number 18: I Stand Alone - reprise (duet)</u>

[Belle] You're not alone, I'm by your side.
Your strength renewed will rise.

[Bob]   I'm not alone,
[Belle] You're not alone,
you're by my side.   I'm
by your side.
My strength renewed will rise.
Your strength renewed will rise.

[The light on Belle fades and she disappears from view.]

Bob: Thank you, dear. Bobbie, do you have any idea how much your mother means to me?

Bobbie: I think I do.

[Lights/curtain down. Fola comes on from the wing.]

Fola: My parents' love for each other always sustained them. Of course, Dad wasn't really alone, or he never could have been elected and re-elected as he was, but often his supporters were not as vocal as his opponents. Bob La Follette sought the Republican nomination for the presidency in 1908, 1912, and 1916, but it was repeatedly denied him. He made no attempt in 1920, when the passions ignited by the war were still too high and he was still fighting for his political life, but in 1924, he accepted the nomination of a third party called the Conference for Progressive Political Action, against the Republican candidate, Calvin Coolidge, and the Democratic candidate, John Davis.

67

Scene 9: La Follette for President

[Campaign workers are milling around, under banners such as "La Follette for President - Wheeler for Vice President", "The Conference for Progressive Political Action Unanimously Endorses La Follette", and "Hull House Welcomes Fighting Bob". Two men and a woman enter.]

Man 1: What's goin' on here.

Woman 1: You don't really expect to have a chance of electin' a president, do you?

Man 2: Especially a radical like La Follette.

Campaign worker: There he is!

[Bob and Belle enter with Jane Addams. Bob is carrying a huge sheaf of paper. The campaign workers give him an enthusiastic welcome, and some of them shake his hand.]

Bob: It is indeed an honor to have a campaign post in Hull House itself, Miss Addams.

Jane Addams: It's we who are honored, Senator. I've been a close friend of your wife for many years -- Belle was there when we formed the Women's Peace Party, and the Women's International League for Peace and Freedom -- and I'm pleased to finally meet the other half of the partnership.

Bob: You may discover that the half you've already met is the better. Maybe I should even let her speak.

Belle: Oh no, they came to hear you.

68

Bob: But I'm so proud of you. No presidential candidate's wife ever went out on the stump before, and you're putting my efforts to shame.

Belle: Don't exaggerate too much.

Jane Addams: And don't you minimize your efforts. You are a credit to our sex, with the organizational work you've done, and your own Chatauqua circuit.

Belle: Jane ... all right, thank you.

Woman 2: What are you going to talk about tonight, Senator?

Bob: I'm going to lay out my entire platform. I plan to talk for three hours. That is, if Miss Addams leaves me any time after her introduction.

Jane Addams: My introduction will be brief. We expect ten thousand people, and they won't be coming to hear me.

Bob: You have no cause to be modest. I shall die content if at the end of my career I feel I have been half as successful as you in the fight for democracy, social justice, equality and decency.

Jane Addams: Thank you, but none of us -- alone -- can address even a fraction of the problems. I am daily appalled by what I see.

<u>Musical Number 19: Can You See Despair?</u>

Can you see despair in the eyes of the children,
their work clothes all covered with soot?

Is each man your brother, each woman your sister,
or are they just dust underfoot?
Will you stretch your hand out to someone who's
        falling,
or will you pretend you don't see?
Will you stretch your hand out to someone who's
        falling,
or will you pretend you don't see?

Can you feel the hunger of earning too little,
the dread of the wintery wind?
Do thick fur coats insulate you from the tempest,
or worse, are you simply thick-skinned.
Will you stretch your hand out to someone who's
        suff'ring,
or will you pretend you're not there?
Will you stretch your hand out to someone who's
        suff'ring,
or will you pretend you're not there?

Can you hear the cries of the sick and the hopeless,
or are they too distant and low?
The rich and the lucky may sing out in pleasure;
The poor and the luckless breathe woe.
Will you stretch your hand out to someone who's
        crying,
or will you pretend you don't hear?
Will you stretch your hand out to someone who's
        crying,
or will you pretend you don't hear?

Man 3: Senator?

Bob: Yes?

Man 3: Could you give us a preview?

Bob: A warm-up? [General enthusuasm.] Well, first I shall tell this audience of ten thousand that they will hear my program for the presidency spelled out in detail, an unprecedented step on the part of a presidential candidate.

[Bob should read most of the following, leafing quickly through his papers, rather than memorize it.] I shall then continue to lament the folly of having gone to war, a war which cost over fifty thousand lives and over two hundred thousand maimed and wounded; which cost over thirty billion dollars, yet to be paid by this generation and future generations; and which cost us the friendship of many great nations with whom we previously had no quarrel and with who knows what consequences for the future: not only Germany and Austria, but Russia and China as well. A war in which, as in all wars, the great mass of people suffered while a favored few profited immensely. A war which by the terms of the Treaty of Versailles has created a condition which is absolutely certain to keep Europe in turmoil and war for years to come. I do not oppose a League of Nations; I proposed one myself in 1915, but I oppose this League of Nations. I do not believe that the president or the state department should have the power, without the knowledge and consent of the Congress or the people, to involve the nation in such a way as to lead to inextricable entanglements, unfavorable commitments or to war. I believe in the democratic control of foreign policy and am unalterably opposed to secret diplomacy. Specifically, if elected, I will endeavor to end our imperialistic attitude toward Central and South America, and to withdraw our Marines from Haiti, Santo Domingo, and every other place where they are now being used to coerce local governments for the benefit of American financiers and special interests.

71

Domestically, those same interests have exploited -- and continue to exploit -- the American laborer and the American farmer. The economic life of eight million American farmers is determined by a handful of men. It is determined by the banking, railroad and exploiting agencies owned by J. P. Morgan and the Standard Oil Company. These are the masters of America. During the years that followed the war, American farmers produced between ten billion and twenty billion dollars worth of wealth, yet the prices they received were fixed by monopolies. The railroads of the country were, and still are, interlaced with the packers, with the millers, with the commission men, and with the grain pits, and together they form an economic system ruled from Wall Street. Unable to meet the production costs from sales, farmers had to go to the banks to borrow to keep alive, and when deflation hit in 1920, more than fifteen hundred banks failed and more than sixty thousand businesses were closed. One million men left the countryside in a single year. Six hundred thousand farmers went bankrupt and gave up their farms.   To attack the symptoms of the problem, I will propose emergency legislation for the relief of agriculture. I propose to reconstruct the Federal Reserve and Federal Farm Loan Systems, so as to make the nation's credit available on fair terms and without discrimination to business men, farmers and home builders. But to attack the causes of the problem, I will initiate a vigorous and honest attempt to enforce the present anti-trust laws, which have never yet been enforced, and I will ... [Bob starts to speak again, but stops, looks around, smiles and relaxes.] A preview, you said? What do you say to giving the real thing to ten thousand people.

[The campaign workers go wild, strike up the campaign song, and eventually follow Bob and Jane Addams off.]

Musical Number 20: Fightin' Bob, The People's Choice

Fightin' Bob, the people's choice,
his the strongest, clearest voice.
Fightin' Bob, the choice is clear;
he's the one our ship of state to steer.

Listen to the words of caution ev'ry pundit says:
Do we really want a Coolidge or a Davis for our
      prez?

Fightin' Bob, the people's choice,
his the strongest, clearest voice.
Fightin' Bob, the choice is clear;
he's the one our ship of state to steer.

Voters of America deserve a better shake.
Electing Tweedledum or Dee or be a huge mistake.

Fightin' Bob, the people's choice,
his the strongest, clearest voice.
Fightin' Bob, the choice is clear;
he's the one our ship of state to steer.

Democrats, Republicans, Progressive members, too,
should cast their votes for Fighting Bob, an honest
      man and true.

Fightin' Bob, the people's choice,
his the strongest, clearest voice.
Fightin' Bob, the choice is clear;
he's the one our ship of state to steer.

[Lights/curtain down. Fola enters with a wheelchair.]

Fola: Robert Marion La Follette lost the election, but he [made the best showing a third-party candidate has ever made.] The loss didn't kill him, but he suffered from remarkably bad health at times, and he didn't live long after that. Why am I the one to be telling you all this? After my father died, my mother turned down the invitation to take his Senate seat, as I told you. Mom continued to be active in numerous causes. She continued to edit La Follette's Weekly Magazine, which later turned into The Progressive. And she began writing a biography of Dad. When she died in 1931, I took on the task of completing that biography, and I finally finished it twenty-two years later, in 1953. You might say I never wanted to let go of either of them. I loved them both very much, and I still do.

Musical Number 21: I Live My Life for Both of You

When I fly on happy wings of mem'ry,
when I smile at who I am today,
then I think of you both evermore.

I remember how you would protect me,
'til you taught me to not be afraid
of the dark and the thunder's roar.

I see you, I feel you, I'll never forget
the love that you gave me, a gift not a debt.

For I know that you'll be always with me,
even when you're not right by my side,
just as you always were before.

I hope you know I'll never let you go.

My heart is where you'll always be;
the two of you are here in me.

I hope you know wherever I may go,
whatever I may say or do,
I live my life for both of you.

Whatever I may say or do,
I live my life for both of you.

[Belle enters.]

Scene 10: Belle and Bob

Fola: Do you think Papa'll be all right?

Belle: I don't know. He's exhausted, and pretty discouraged right now. You know how fragile his health has always been. He's always suffered terribly from headaches and stomach problems, especially when he's campaigning. You remember, when you were eighteen, when he was governor and his first legislative program was defeated --

Fola: How could I forget. We thought he might never get out of bed again. It lasted a year, didn't it?

Belle: Very nearly. He's come through times like this before, but I'm always afraid that someday he'll really overtax himself. We just have to be as positive as we can.

Bob: As positive about what as you can. Me?

[Bob enters. Fola hugs and kisses him on the cheek, and he kisses her back. He sits.]

Belle: Your health.

Bob: Fola, how are you.

Fola: I'm fine, Papa. How are you?

Bob: I'm ... you know, we've always made it a point to be truthful with each other ... I'm not well at all. But having you here has lifted my spirits out of the cellar, at least. How's this new show you're in?

Fola: It's doing fine. We had full houses last weekend.

Will you come to see it?

Bob: I wouldn't miss it for the world.

Belle: We already have our tickets.

Bob: Your show's more successful than mine. Oh, don't exchange worried looks. I can still joke, especially about my old love, the theater, but I am feeling very tired.

Fola: I'll leave you alone. I just wanted to come by and say hello and let you know I love you.

Bob: I love you, too. Oh, before you go, how's George's new play coming along.

Fola: Not as well as it should. He says he's hit a roadblock, which means a mental block, but I think I can help him with it, and I'm confident he'll meet his deadline.

Belle: You two are so lucky to have each other and to share so much.

Fola: Just like you two. We're merely following in your footsteps, a founder of the Women's Peace Party, and --

Bob: And a failed presidential candidate.

Fola: Daddy, --   **Belle:** Bob --

Bob: I'm sorry. I am feeling ... melancholy. Is your husband still happy with your decision to keep your own last name?

Fola: You bet. And if he wasn't, I wouldn't've married him.

He is the most supportive man alive. That's another way in which he and I are like you and Mama. [Who else would've taken the word "obey" out of their marriage vows back then.

Bob: That was her idea, though I'm glad she did. Because if we hadn't agreed to get rid of it, the alternative was for me to vow to obey her.]

Fola: Right, Daddy. [Fola kisses and hugs both Bob and Belle.] You look like you could use some rest. George and I'll stop by on Sunday. Bye.

Bob: Bye.

Belle: Good-bye, dear.

Bob: I'm so proud of her.

Belle: She's always been your daughter.

Bob: Even if she was ... a few weeks early.

Belle: No-one's ever faulted you or me for that.

Bob: If only they'd known. Belle, I am tired --

Belle: How about --

Bob: and I can't get over the feeling that I failed. I failed the American public, and I failed you.

Belle: You did not! You lost an election. You've lost elections before, and got over them, and kept trying until you won.

Bob: I'm old.

Belle: So am I. We get that way.

Bob: But I'm sixty-nine. That's old. I won't be able to do this again.

Belle: I don't understand. When you were defeated for re-election in 1890, you never spoke one word of complaint, you never frowned once. You said life was too important to let the vagaries of politics spoil it.

Bob: I'm not well.

Belle: You've always driven yourself too hard. And you've always recovered. [Do you remember the press release I wrote for you after you got so exhausted during the campaign? "On occasion, when his zeal to battle privilege has overtaxed his strength, he has had to stop, but he always recuperated and returned to the field with renewed vigor. We who know him realize that he will never relinquish the fight as long as he lives."] Let's relax for awhile.

Bob: Belle, I'm afraid ...

Belle: Of what.

Bob: This time I'm afraid if I relax I may die. [Beat. She goes to hold his hand.] You and I've done well, though, haven't we, except for this last election.

Belle: Just running in this election was a great victory, and you know it.

Bob: You know what my favorite time was?

79

Belle: When.

Bob: When we were governor. Everything seemed possible then.

Belle: And much of it happened just as you worked for it to happen.

Bob: Our children are wonderful, aren't they.

Belle: They certainly are.

Bob: You've been a wonderful mother. If Fola married the most supportive man alive, I married the most supportive woman alive.

Belle: That's not it. We've always been partners. La Follette and La Follette. I've had just as much opportunity to work for the good of the country as you have, and you've been just as good a parent as I have.

Bob: It's been a long time since I saw the tall pines and the wild places.

Musical Number 22: Bob and Belle

(Bob) Here in the dusk of my day
wondering what it's all worth,
tired and bruised from the fray,
soon to return to the earth.

(Belle) Knowing you're still here beside me,
comforting me as you do,

80

I'm grateful that you've helped to guide me,
My happiest strength has been with you.

(Bob) You on whom I've relied
when faced with the toughest demand.
(Belle) You who've walked by my side,
facing each day hand-in-hand.

(Together, as in reprise in scene 3)
(Belle) My choice has always been clear.
I found myself in us.
Now we two have lived as peers.
I gave to you all of my love.
We knew what to do, my love.
(Bob) We've been together.
Your dreams and my dreams we worked to unite.
You were my choice.
Now I know in my choice I was right.
I gave to you all of my love.
We knew what to do, my love.

[The scene changes back to the funeral.]

Brandeis: He was defeated for the presidency. That means his name will not appear as often in the history books as that of those who achieve that office, so it is inevitable that his name will be forgotten more quickly, but Robert La Follette has had a greater impact on the social and political life of his state and his country than that of almost all of his contemporaries, and almost all of us standing here today.

No leader among us, not a Roosevelt, a Taft, a Wilson, a Harding, or a Coolidge, has been praised more extravagantly by his supporters or vilified more vehemently by his enemies. If you stand still for a moment, and listen carefully, you can almost hear the collective sigh of relief being breathed in the country today by the barons of wealth and the lords of monopoly.

Fighting Bob La Follette was a man of unimpeachable integrity and unassailable courage. I am proud to have called him my friend. And when I meet him again in the afterlife, for [I believe in it] even if he didn't -- he's probably surprised to be there right now, and he's probably discussing the perilous state of the union with his peers there: Washington, Jefferson, and Lincoln -- I will walk up to him and shake his hand and tell him, even in front of those others, that I never knew a greater American.

<u>Musical Number 23: If (choral setting)</u>

If you can talk with crowds and keep your virtue,
Or walk with Kings -- nor lose the common touch,
If neither foes nor loving friends can hurt you,
If all men count with you, but none too much;

If you can fill the unforgiving minute
With sixty seconds' worth of distance run,
Yours is the Earth and everything that's in it,
And -- which is more -- you'll be a Man, you'll be a
        man, my son, you'll be a man.

You'll be a man.
You'll be a man.
You'll be a man.

        END

The Saga of Sergeant Bates

dramatization by John Schweitzer
4713 Regent Street
Madison, WI 53705
608-231-3941

based on research by John Vorndran
copyright 2002-3

<u>Scenes</u>

Curtain Music to Act I

Act I

1. The End and the Beginning
2. Sergeant Bates's Bet
3. Hard Times
4. Breaking the News
5. Half Twain
6. Vicksburg, Part I
7. Vicksburg, Part II
8. Sending the News Home, Part I

Intermission

Curtain Music to Act II

Act II

9. On the Road
10. Southern Hospitality
11. A Warning
12. Sending the News Home, Part II
13. A Soldier's Soul
14. Homeward Bound
15. The End of the Journey

Cast (in order of appearance)

John Sorenson, a shop-owner in Edgerton
Bill Carter, owner of the Edgerton General Store
Sergeant Gilbert Bates
Gabriel, a Southern soldier
Sarah, Gabriel's wife
Calvin, Gabriel's son
Milly, Gabriel's daughter
Ann E., Bates's wife
Hattie, Bates's daughter
Arthur Colfax, Reporter
Frank Howard
Charles Washburn, Mayor of Vicksburg
Mrs. Pemberton
Mrs. Partridge
Mrs. Parker
First Man or Woman in crowd
Second Man or Woman in crowd
Third Man or Woman in crowd
Man at railroad crossing
Mr. Ward, plantation owner
Mrs. Ward
George Sanders, former Southern soldier
A Man in Augusta, Georgia
Peter Thomas, an African American in Augusta
Other soldiers, former soldiers, and citizens.

==

Curtain Music to Act I

*[By printing the words in the program, etc., encourage the
audience to sing.]*

Shenandoah
Oh, Shenandoah, I long to hear you,
Away, you rolling river.
Oh, Shenandoah, just to be near you,
Away, we're bound away, 'cross the wide Missouri.

Aura Lee
As the blackbird in the spring, beneath the willow tree,
Sat and piped, I heard him sing, sing "Aura Lee".
Aura Lee, Aura Lee, maid of golden hair!
Sunshine came along with thee, and swallows in the air.

==

==

Act I

Scene I: The End and the Beginning

*["Dixie's Land" should be sung, if possible, by males in
Confederate uniform.]*

ONE OR MORE SOUTHERN SOLDIERS
I wish I was in the de land ob cotton, Old times dar am not
forgotten,
Look away, Look away! Look away! Dixie Land.
In Dixie Land whar I was born in, Early on one frosty
mornin,
Look away! Look away! Look away! Dixie Land.
Den I wish I was in Dixie, Hooray! Hooray!
In Dixie Land, I'll took my stand, To lib an die in Dixie,
Away, Away, Away down south in Dixie,
Away, Away, Away down south in Dixie.

*[The "Battle Hymn of the Republic" should be sung, if
possible, by males in Union uniform standing at attention.
While it is being sung, Confederate soldiers walk past, stack
their rifles and walk off. Gabriel limps on in a particularly
ragged uniform, adds his rifle to the stack, steps back and
tearfully salutes his rifle. He then salutes the nearest Union
soldier and limps off.]*

ONE OR MORE NORTHERN SOLDIERS
Mine eyes have seen the glory of the coming of the lord;
He is trampling out the vintage where the grapes of wrath are
stored;
He hath loosed the fateful lightning of his terrible swift
sword;
His truth is marching on.
Glory! Glory hallelujah! Glory! Glory! Glory hallelujah!
Glory! Glory hallelujah! His truth is marching on.

89

Scene 2. Sergeant Bates's Bet
The main street in Edgerton, Wisconsin
November 1867

[Lights up. At center stage is the facade of the general store. At one edge of the stage is the railroad depot. On the covered portico of the general store, two men, John and Bill, are sitting, playing checkers. Bill has a newspaper on his lap. Bates enters.]

BATES
Good mornin', Bill, John.

[Bill stands and salutes him, a mixture of respect, habit and camaraderie.]

BILL
Sergeant Bates.

JOHN
Howdy, Gilbert.

BATES
I've told you before, just Mister Bates now, if you please.

BILL
You'll always be Sergeant Bates to me.

BATES
Isn't it strange how war turns things upside-down. Here you are, still salutin' me, when you're older 'n' wiser, 'n' I do believe a sight richer than I am, as owner of the most successful general store in Edgerton.

JOHN
The only general store in Edgerton.

BILL
Now, now. If it weren't up to snuff, there'd be another one

90

here. What brings you to town.

BATES
I brought my scythes in for sharpening, now that the harvest
is all in. What's the news in the "Union".

JOHN
It looks like the Radical Republicans in Congress is gettin'
ready to impeach President Johnson.

BATES
What for.

JOHN
For high crimes and misdemeanors.

BATES
And what do they think that means?

BILL
Well, you know he replaced Secretary of War Stanton with
General Grant.

BATES
That's a crime?

JOHN
Johnson's a Southerner!

BATES
Is that a crime? He's a loyal Southerner from Tennessee, the
only Southern Senator to renounce secession, chosen by
Lincoln himself for Vice President.

JOHN
Well, even Lincoln wasn't perfect, now was he? Johnson's a
wolf in sheep's clothing.

BATES
He's doin' just what Lincoln would 'a' done. He's tryin' t'
carry' out Lincoln's policies toward the South.

JOHN
Well, Lincoln was wrong about that, too. If he'd lived past
the end o' the war, he would 'a' changed his tune. Gilbert,
tryin' t' reconstruct the South's a lost cause. It'll never
happen, 'cause the South's unreconstructable.

BATES
I don't want to get into an argument with you, John. You
know how I feel.

JOHN
If you hadn't enlisted, I'd almost think you were a Southern
sympathizer.

BATES
Bill, before I forget, do you have any more o' that elixir, the
stuff in the brown bottles? Our Hattie's been feverish with
catarrh for a couple o' days now, and my wife asked me to
pick up a bottle. It worked last time Hattie was feelin'
poorly.

BILL
Just one?

BATES
Just one. Money's pretty tight this time o' year.

BILL
This whole year. That'll be two bits.

[Bill hands him a bottle in return for the coins.]

BATES
Thank you.

BILL
Do you want to leave your scythes here? I can get 'em done in a couple of days.

BATES
Same price as last year?

BILL
Yep.

BATES
All right with me. I left 'em around back.

[A distant train whistle is heard, followed by the distant sound of a train that passes through without stopping.]

JOHN
There's the two-twenty. Do you have anything on it?

BILL
Nope.

JOHN
Nope, doesn't sound like it's stoppin'. Say, did you know Corporal Cooper died?

BATES
No, when.

BILL
Sam Wilkins told me that yesterday.

JOHN
It says here he died on Sunday after a long battle with neuralgia, and the flag'll be flown at half-mast over the courthouse for a week startin' today to honor him. Did you serve with him?

BATES
No, he was with the Sixth Wisconsin, in the Iron Brigade. I did meet him once, on the train coming home from Washington. He fought at Antietam. I still remember the story he told of that day. He was a splendid man and a right officer.

JOHN
Was he a Radical?

BATES
I don't remember that we talked about political views. But he fought when he was needed. He deserves a flag at half-mast.

JOHN
You won't see an American flag at half-mast anywhere in the South. You won't see it at full mast, for that matter, except where there are Union troops.

BATES
You're wrong.

JOHN
Gilbert, the Southerners are rebels yet. They're worse now than they were during the war. They hate the Union flag. Why, if someone tried to fly it in the South, it'd be torn down. No man would dare show that flag anywhere in the South except in the presence of armed soldiers.

BATES
You're wrong. The Southerners have accepted the outcome of the conflict and they want to get on with their lives. The flag is as honored there as it is here.

JOHN
Ha! You don't know what you're talkin' about.

BATES
Yes, I do. I could fly that flag myself in any of the former
Confederate states.

JOHN
And if you did, the Rebels'd cut your heart out and tear your
flag to pieces and trample it in the dust.

BATES
You do the South a great wrong to say that. The Southern
people are just as willing to live in the Union as we are.
You're wrong, and I'd be willing to prove it.

JOHN
Prove it? How would you prove it.

[Beat.]

BATES
As I just said, I'll fly the flag myself, in any Southern city
you choose. You buy me passage and I'll unfurl Old Glory
in the town square -- the regimental standard I still have at
home -- and I'll hear more cheers than catcalls.

JOHN
It won't be a matter of catcalls. You'll have to have a cat's
lives, 'cause it'll be your life in your hands.

BATES
You suffer from the illusion that we're still at war.

JOHN
It's you who suffer from an illusion, some romantic illusion
that the Southerners have reformed. Southerners killed my
boy at Gettysburg. They hate the North and the Union, and
defeat just makes 'em hate us more. I'd take your wager
gladly, but I don't wish to be the cause of your untimely

demise.

BATES
Have no fear on that account. Let's make the wager worth the winning. I'll prove it across the whole South.

JOHN
What do you mean.

BATES
I'll carry the flag from one end to the other.

JOHN
You're out of your mind.

BATES
I believe in the people of the South.

BILL
You talk as if they're Christian saints.

BATES
No, I just trust them to be like people everywhere.

BILL
Sergeant, people aren't like that everywhere, maybe not anywhere.

JOHN
It goes against human nature to accept defeat.

BILL
What's human nature.

JOHN
Avenging wrongs and insults and defeats.

BILL

Human nature's much more than that ...

BATES
Now don't get into a philosophical debate. I just know what
I know.

JOHN
And I know what I know, and they'll kill you!

BATES
No, they won't. The war is over!

JOHN
They killed Lincoln after the war was over.

[Pause.]

BATES
Booth was just one man.

JOHN
It would only take one man.

[Slight pause.]

BATES
Passions were still high then.

BILL
Gilbert, you can't do it. Do you want to get killed?

BATES
I'll do it. I'll carry the flag. What do you put up against that.

[Long pause.]

JOHN
I hesitate, but not from fear of losing, only from fear of

winning.

BATES
You made the challenge. Now make good on it.

JOHN
Gilbert, I don't like this.

BATES
I insist. I'm calling your bluff.

JOHN
If I thought you could do it, I'd gladly pay your passage. I just want it to be live passage and not freight. And if you were to return alive, a dollar a day for every day you spend on the road with the flag.

BATES
Done!

BILL
Are you talkin' about walkin'?

BATES
Yes.

BILL
Why not just take the train.

BATES
What would be the point of that.

BILL
Well, you could stop at every town.

BATES
Nope. It wouldn't be the same at all.

BILL
But would you leave your wife and child? again?

BATES
I will. This is the fallow season. If I start soon, I figure I
can walk from the Mississippi to the Potomac in three
months. My fields are ready for plantin' in the spring, and I
can return by the time I'm needed. A dollar a day's a lot
more than I can make sittin' here. Besides, I left them for
the war, and they fared. My wife is as good in the field as a
man. She managed by herself last year, with the horse --
Thank goodness they didn't have to take Chestnut for the
war. -- and she could do it again if she had to. But she won't
have to; I'll be back by then.

BILL
Sergeant, if you ever set foot in South Carolina, you'll never
come out again unless it's in a coffin.

BATES
You'll eat those words.

BILL
I wish I could believe you were right.

BATES
Well?

JOHN
I hate sendin' a man to his death, but ... if that's what you
want, it's a wager. *[He holds out his hand.]* But you have to
explain to your wife and everyone else that you're the one
who got you into this. I don't want them blamin' me.

[They shake hands.]

BATES
All right! You're the witness.

BILL

You're touched, but it's a noble cause. I hope you're right. I can take care of your food. I could send you off with enough for a couple of weeks, and resupply you along the way.

BATES

Thank you, Bill, but no. I can find hospitality there, as I would here.

BILL

You don't need to make this trip harder 'n it already is.

BATES

I don't want to travel with a supply train, like an armed camp.

JOHN

Well, you will have to go armed. What will you carry.

[Long pause while Bates considers this.]

BATES

Nothing. Would I feel the need to carry weapons on a hike from Edgerton to Stoughton?

JOHN

Don't be a fool! The road to Stoughton isn't hostile territory.

BATES

And neither is the road from Vicksburg to Washington.

[Lights down.]

===

Scene 3. Hard Times
Outside a cabin in North Carolina
November 1867

*[Lights up. Gabriel, the soldier who was seen stacking his
rifle, still limping, plays "Hard Times" on a fiddle or a
concertina while Sarah, his wife, sings. A young boy
(Calvin) and a young girl (Milly) listen and may sing along.
The wooden cross of Scene 10 is present, but the lighting
makes it almost invisible.]*

SARAH
Let us pause in life's pleasures and count its many tears,
While we all sup sorrow with the poor,
There's a song that will linger forever in our ears.
Oh! Hard times, come again no more.
'Tis the song, the sigh of the weary:
Hard times, hard times come again no more.
Many days you have lingered around my cabin door.
Oh! Hard times, come again no more.

GABRIEL
The fella who wrote that sure knew his stuff.

SARAH
Even though the word's 's so sad, I love to hear it. Music's
one o' the few beautiful things we have left, besides each
other.

GABRIEL
Ain't much else, 'n' it jus' don't get better. Two 'n' a half
years. You think we c'n survive this winter?

SARAH
Like last year. Yes. There won't be much, but if we're
careful, we'll eat. D' you suppose there'll be any chance o'

101

gettin' a horse 'r a mule next year? The plantin's hard without Nell. I was so sad when I heard she was killed. We could plant more.

GABRIEL
Even if we could find one f'r sale -- 'n' I don't think there're more than five left in the whole county -- what could we buy it with.

SARAH
The black folks keep sayin' the Freedmen's Bureau's gonna give 'em all forty acres 'n' a mule. D' you suppose there's any way we could get one f'r ourselves while they're gettin' 'em? We're as bad off as any o' them.

GABRIEL
I don' know. The Freedmen's Bureau ain't f'r helpin' us. It don't seem like they're helpin' much of anybody, but least of all us poor white folks. At least we got this, 'n' we got our family, all together here. Besides, all that 'bout forty acres 'n' a mule was jus' somethin' General Sherman said when he marched t' the sea, 'n' it don' seem t' be happenin'. The North is rulin' the Old South like a conquered country, 'n' they ain't lettin' up. I jus' wish ...

[Pause.]

SARAH
What.

GABRIEL
Nothin'. I jus' wish I could do somethin'.

SARAH
There's nothin' any of us c'n do. Everyone's as bad off 's we are, 'n' some a sight worse. I see enough widows when I go t' town to know just how lucky I am. At least you're here to help with the crops --

GABRIEL
Such as they are.

SARAH
And the children. At least we're all together. We should be thankful.

GABRIEL
Thankful? Yes, but it's hard.

[Lights down.]

===

Scene 4. Breaking the News
Outside a farmhouse in Albion Township, Wisconsin
November 1867

[Ann E. and Hattie are sitting together. Hattie holds a rag doll as she watches Ann E. sewing.]

ANN E.
This is the way we mend our clothes, mend our clothes, mend our --

HATTIE
Papa! You're back!

BATES
Hey there, Hattie. Hello, darlin'.

ANN E.
Hello, dear.

BATES
My, my, you both just look prettier every time I see you.

ANN E.
Now stop it. I understood when you said that after you returned from the war, but isn't it about time you got used to us again.

BATES
I don't ever want to get used to you, or take either one of you for granted. I missed you too much when I was away, 'n' I still get that feelin' when I leave you, even to go to town.

ANN E.
Well, then, just don't go away again ... ever.

[Beat.]

HATTIE
Do you know what happened while you were gone?

BATES
What.

HATTIE
Calico had kittens!

BATES
You don't say! How many did she have.

HATTIE
Five! Do you want to see 'em?

BATES
I sure do, but I need to talk to your mother first. What color are they.

HATTIE
All different colors!

BATES
You don't say. Why don't you go and take another look at 'em.

HATTIE
You bet!

ANN E
Don't touch 'em yet! And don't get too close to Calico! She won't like it if you do.

[Hattie runs off.]

ANN E

What do we need to talk about.

BATES
Well, it's ... it's funny you should say that about not leavin' again.

[Pause.]

ANN E.
What's funny about it.

BATES
Well, maybe it isn't funny. It's actually pretty serious.

ANN E
You're leaving? Why. Where.

BATES
Well, you know, we talked about this before. A lot o' people still think the worst about Southerners and, just like the Radicals in Washington, they want to keep 'em out o' the Union as long as possible, it seems. *[Pause.]* Do you remember you asked me if I ever saw President Lincoln when I was in Washington?

ANN E
I did, and you didn't have a chance to answer me. I remember. Did you?

BATES
Yes. Sometimes I saw him from a distance when he'd review the troops, and I'd just catch a glimpse of him as we marched past -- It was hard to miss him. -- but I did get to see him real close once. He was speaking at the Capitol and the public was invited and I was off duty, so I went real early and got a good place up front. I've never seen a man of fifty-six look so old. I can still see him in my mind's eye, and I remember most of what he said.

106

ANN E
Was that the speech you sent me?

BATES
Yes. His Second Inaugural Address.

ANN E
I read it, over and over. It was so inspiring. I read it out
loud to Hattie, but she didn't understand much of it.

BATES
I haven't thought about that for a long time now. Do you
still have it?

ANN E
Of course. Do you want me to get it? *[Bates nods his
head.]* All right. I know right where it is. I put it with your
letters. *[She exits and returns quickly, while Bates sits either
fidgeting nervously or looking pensive.]* Here it is.

BATES
Would you read it to me?

ANN E.
You want me to read it, out loud?

BATES
If you would. Just those parts I underlined when I sent it to
you.

ANN E
Fellow-Countrymen: ... On the occasion corresponding to
this four years ago all thoughts were anxiously directed to an
impending civil war. ... Both parties deprecated war, but
one of them would *make* war rather than let the nation
survive, and the other would *accept* war rather than let it
perish, and the war came. ... Neither party expected for the

war the magnitude or the duration which it ... attained. ...
Both read the same Bible and [prayed] to the same God, and
each [invoked] His aid against the other. ... With malice
toward none, with charity for all, with firmness in the right
as God gives us to see the right, let us strive on to finish the
work we are in, to bind up the nation's wounds, to care for
him who shall have borne the battle and for his widow and
his orphan, to do all which may achieve and cherish a just
and lasting peace among ourselves and with all nations.

BATES
Lincoln never hated the South. Despite everything, he loved
the South, as you'd love a wayward child. Did I ever tell you
that the very night Lee surrendered, a band went to serenade
Lincoln and they asked him what tune he'd like to hear. Did
I tell you this?

ANN E
No.

BATES
Do you know what tune he asked them to play?

ANN E
No, what.

BATES
He asked 'em to play "Dixie". He said it was a right good
tune, 'n' one of his favorites. He said it'd been gone too long,
and he was glad to have it back in the Union again. *[Long
pause.]* Like a wayward child. So anyway, I got into a ... a
discussion with John in Bill's store, 'n' .... *[Pause.]* You
know, things are pretty well taken care of here on the farm
right now. Winter's comin' on, 'n' there won't be any hard
work 'til spring. I took care of most everything that needed
fixin', 'n' it looks like there won't be much to do for a few
months. *[Long pause.]* So John'n' I got to talkin' about
Southerners, and since it's the off season and all, well, what I

108

did was take a wager that'll earn me a dollar a day in the off season.

ANN E.
A dollar a day! That's grand! But where do you have to go.
And it's a wager, not a job?

BATES
Yep.

ANN E.
What's the wager. You didn't bet the farm!

BATES
No!

ANN E
Well, what happens if you lose the bet.

BATES
Then I might not be comin' back.

ANN E.
What?!

BATES
John bet me I couldn't show the flag anywhere in the South
safely, 'n' I bet him I could.

ANN E.
You took a bet that you could show the flag in the South.
Where would you go. We don't have the money for you to
go South, even to Memphis.

BATES
He'll take care o' that. He'll pay my fare, and he'll pay me a
dollar a day while I'm ... while I'm away.

ANN E
All right. Where are you planning to go, and when.

BATES
Well, I plan to start in Vicksburg.

ANN E
Start?

BATES
Well, the actual bet was that I could carry the flag across the entire South, on foot and unarmed.

ANN E
No! You aren't serious.

BATES
I'm afraid I am, darlin'.

ANN E
Walk?

BATES
Walkin' is one thing I can do.

ANN E
Gilbert ....

BATES
What.

ANN E
Walk across the entire South? Alone, on foot, unarmed?

BATES
I can do it.

ANN E.

For how long.

BATES
I figure a couple of months, maybe three. I figure I can walk
twenty miles a day, easy, and Vicksburg to Washington is
'bout fourteen hundred miles. Seventy days.

ANN E.
Right now?

BATES
Well, we didn't work out that detail. Winter may not be the
best time for weather, but it'd be the best time for you here
on the farm. Maybe when we figure you can best spare me.

ANN E.
Gilbert, you'll ... you're ...

BATES
John said the Southerners're still rebels, 'n' I said he's wrong:
they're ready to rejoin the Union. You and I talked about
that.

ANN E.
Yes, we did, and I agree with you, but even if you're right, it
would take only one angry man to ... to keep you from
comin' home. Don't do it! You can cancel the wager, can't
you?

BATES
I don't want to.

ANN E.
You can't do it!

BATES
Don't you understand? It's important to me to do something
to heal this country. It's just for two or three months.

ANN E
The two or three months I could handle. That isn't what I'm
worried about. Just one disgruntled veteran. You don't want
to leave us ... alone. It's dangerous.

BATES
I know that, but three million men took that chance during
the war.

ANN E
And one out of five never came back.

BATES
I did.

[Hattie runs back on.]

HATTIE
Papa! You've got to come and see! They opened their eyes!

BATES
I'm coming!

[Bates exits, leaving Ann E. Lights down.]

===

===

Scene 5. Half Twain
On a Mississippi River boat
January 1868

[The sound of a (paddle-wheel) boat steaming through the water. The stage is dimly lit. A few lanterns and chairs represent the deck of the boat. Arthur Colfax and Frank Howard are sitting next to each other, dressed for winter.]

VOICE OFFSTAGE
Half twain!

FRANK HOWARD
River sure is beautiful tonight, ain't it.

ARTHUR COLFAX
If you like broken glass piled up along the shores.

HOWARD
What? Why sure enough. The ice does look like that, doesn't it. Makes it seem even prettier.

COLFAX
And the sentries on either shore? faceless and gaunt?

[Pause.]

HOWARD
The trees? Not as beautiful as they are in the spring or the summer, or the fall for that matter, but they're still part of a great beautiful night.

COLFAX
Beauty is in the eye of the beholder. Personally, my idea of beauty a thunderstorm as it bears down over the prairie

HOWARD
Well, no storm tonight. Just look at the sky. There's
somethin' about the air in winter. It's clearer, or deeper.
You can see every star ever made.

COLFAX
And every one o' those stars is lookin' back at us thinkin'
"what is man comin' to".

*[Bates enters, wearing comfortable nondescript clothes
without a coat, carrying his furled flag and his pack.]*

BATES
Good evenin'.

COLFAX and HOWARD
Good evening.

BATES
Mind if I join you gentlemen?

HOWARD
Come ahead, sir. That chair's free.

COLFAX
As is the view to eternity.

[Bates takes the chair next to them.]

HOWARD
Where're you headed?

BATES
Vicksburg. And you ?

COLFAX
New Orleans. *[He pronounces it as written.]*

114

HOWARD
Memphis. Next stop. But Vicksburg's my home. I'll be
headin' there by land after I get off. May even get there
before you do. What's your business there, 'n' does it have
anything to do with that flag you're totin'?

BATES
It has everything to do with the flag. I plan to fly it in
Vicksburg and across the South.

HOWARD
Is it the ... Stars and Stripes?

BATES
Yep. In point of fact, it's my regimental flag from the war.

COLFAX
And what asylum did you escape from.

BATES
I beg your pardon, sir. What did you say?

COLFAX
I asked what asylum you escaped from.

BATES
Did you intend that as a jest or an insult.

COLFAX
As a madman, you may take it any way you wish.

BATES
I'm not in the habit of being addressed as a madman.

COLFAX
I, on the other hand, seem to have fallen into the habit of
addressing madmen wherever I go, especially during the past
eight years of war and reconstruction.

115

HOWARD
You must have a purpose for this, sir

BATES
I do. I intend to show that the South needs no further
reconstruction at Northern hands, and that its citizens are
ready, even eager, to get on with their lives by rejoining the
Union and swearing their allegiance to its banner.

COLFAX
So when do we get to see your other banner.

BATES
Sir? Is that another insult, to me or to the flag?

COLFAX
This may be the banner you show openly, but you must also
be carrying a banner for the politician who commissioned
you, and the only person I can think of with the gall to do
something like this would be our unfortunate President. But
how would you know King Andy. Your accent is from
somewhere far to the north of Tennessee.

BATES
I am no person's hireling and I resent your baseless insults.
What is your name, sir.

COLFAX
Colfax. Arthur Colfax. Perhaps you've heard of it or read it
as a byline in one of the better newspapers.

BATES
Perhaps I haven't. My accent is from Wisconsin, where I
farm in the township of Albion and read the Edgerton Union,
which I suspect fails to qualify as one of the better
newspapers, precisely because it does not carry your articles.
[To Frank Howard.] I'll take my leave of you, sir.

116

HOWARD
Your name, please, before you go. I have a feeling I'll be
hearing it again.

BATES
Gilbert Bates. And yours?

HOWARD
Frank Howard.

BATES
Mister Howard, I wish we had met under more favorable
circumstances, but I feel it would be better if I move on.

HOWARD
Good luck.

BATES
Thank you.

[Bates exits. Long pause.]

HOWARD
I'm curious. Do you always make it your business to be so
caustic?

COLFAX
When I see folly, I call it for what it is.

HOWARD
You think there's no possibility his motive's genuine.

COLFAX
No sane man embraces certain death to prove a point.

HOWARD
And what makes you say it's certain death to show the flag in

117

Vicksburg.

[Beat.]

COLFAX
Would you repeat the question?

HOWARD
What makes you say it's certain death to show the Stars and Stripes in Vicksburg.

COLFAX
I never thought before now that madness was catching.

HOWARD
Now that it's turned on me, I too resent your tone. Your cynicism blinds you. He's not insane. Audacious, but not insane.

COLFAX
He's trying to get himself killed, to be a martyr for some mysterious cause, something I don't understand. To end Reconstruction single-handedly? Is that sane?

HOWARD
I admit I don't understand it, but I think he's on to something.

COLFAX
Are you saying he can traverse the South with that flag and live? Are you forgetting that every night in their sleep [a hundred] thousand Southern veterans still sight their rifles at blue uniforms?

HOWARD
And are you forgetting that as long as the people at the North think that, the South will have to endure military governments, Freedmen's Bureaus, and all the other oppressions of Reconstruction?

118

COLFAX
I have no regard for Reconstruction. It is a spectacular
failure, which deserves abolition as much as the South's
other peculiar institution did, but do you expect him to put
an end to it?

HOWARD
No, not singlehandedly, but if you feel that way, why not
help him. I hardly need tell you how influential the press is
in forming and changing public opinion, even more
influential than a man with a flag. A man's first response to
him might be skepticism, or ridicule or scorn, or even
violence, but if the people can be led to contemplate what
he's really doing, if he were to succeed in his march ...

COLFAX
You want to use him for your own purposes.

HOWARD
Why not. Why not help him. His purpose -- whatever it is --
coincides with the South's purpose, and if the level heads of
the South can see what his march means before the hot heads
do what they do best ...

COLFAX
Are you serious? Do you think there's ant possibility of
reconciliation?

HOWARD
There has to be.

COLFAX
As you seem to have noticed, I have a highly-refined sense
of realism, or as you would have it, cynicism. But perhaps
there is a chance, just a chance, since there was one quality
this war lacked.

HOWARD
What was that.

COLFAX
Inhuman cruelty. Neither side routinely tortured or
mutilated or raped the other, as in religious wars the world
over. Despite all the death and destruction, both sides
seemed to realize that the others were almost brothers, and
that non-combatants were still human. I traveled to Europe
not long ago, and one of the most horrifying sights ...

VOICE OFFSTAGE
Memphis! Prepare lines! Comin' to dock at Memphis!

HOWARD
Excuse me, I must get ready to depart. Have a pleasant trip
to New Orleans. *[He pronounces it "nyawlins".]* Or would
you rather I wish you an unpleasant trip.

COLFAX
I'll settle for uneventful: no burst boilers, no submerged
snags to rip the bottom out of the boat, and no more
visionary volunteers.

HOWARD
Hang onto that cheerful thought. Good-bye.

COLFAX
Good-bye.

[Frank Howard exits. Lights down.]

==

==

Scene 6. Vicksburg, Part I
Vicksburg, Mississippi
January 23, 1868

[Lights up slightly. The stage is dark and somehow frightening. Dim outlines of buildings may be seen. Bates enters carrying his regimental flag furled and covered. He may also be carrying either a small haversack or a pouch on a shoulder strap. He is clearly uncertain and just a little scared. Bates looks around, trying to decide what to do. The lights from one and then many torches begin to make ominous shadows, then voices and indistinct shouts are heard. Bates does not exhibit fear, but he straightens up to a military bearing to meet whatever is coming.]

VOICES
There he is! Come on, boys!

[A small group of men enters and stops a few feet from Bates. They mass in an uncertain attitude, and this should be drawn out as long as possible. Finally, one of them separates from the mass and comes forward with hand outstretched.]

HOWARD
Sergeant Bates!

BATES
Mister Howard. I'm sure glad to see you!

HOWARD
Welcome to Vicksburg! Welcome to Mississippi and the South.

BATES
I'm truly pleased to be here.

121

[Lights up as torches come on. When everyone is onstage it is apparent that the crowd includes a few Northern as well as Southern uniforms.]

HOWARD
Is this the flag?

BATES
It is.

HOWARD
Could you uncover and unfurl it?

BATES
With pleasure. *[He takes off a cover and unfurls a weather-beaten flag with 36 stars.]* This is what I came here for. It was my regiment's banner.

[The unfurling causes the crowd to become very still. It is a moment charged with memories and emotions. Bates too becomes quiet and thoughtful. Finally one of the Union veterans salutes the flag. Others follow, including some, and then all, of the Southern veterans. One drops to his knee and bows his head. Frank Howard and others place their hands on their hearts. Bates looks around, with tears in his eyes.]

BATES
The flag is no small thing.

[Long pause.]

HOWARD
But ... where's your baggage, where are your traveling clothes?

BATES
I have nothing but what you see.

HOWARD
We'll have to see what we can do about that. I bring an
invitation from the Mayor of Vicksburg to attend a
celebration the day after tomorrow in the town square in
honor of you and your flag. Tonight and tomorrow night
you will be my guest at the Prentiss House.

BATES
That's very kind of you.

*[Bates begins to furl the flag and the crowd goes silent
again. When he finishes, he shakes hands with everyone.]*

HOWARD
If you please, Sergeant Bates.

*[Howard leads Bates off and the others follow. Lights
down.]*

===

Scene 7. Vicksburg, Part II
Vicksburg, Mississippi
January 25, 1868

*[Lights up. The set can be the same as the last scene of Act
I, but in the light of day it is a festive town square. The
curtain rises on the mayor, Frank Howard, other prominent
citizens, and Gilbert Bates on a raised dais or bandstand.
The crowd includes Southern soldiers, Northern soldiers,
and women.]*

MAYOR CHARLES WASHBURN
Ladies and gentlemen of Vicksburg, it is my privilege to
introduce to you a man who has taken upon himself the
monumental task of demonstrating that the two great powers
that inflicted untold death, pain, suffering and devastation on
each other in the recent war, are reconciled and once again
joined as partners and as brethren. That man is Gilbert
Bates, who is now, like most of us, a private citizen, but who
three years ago was a Sergeant in the First Wisconsin Heavy
Artillery. Sergeant, the citizens of Vicksburg and I applaud
your purpose and your resolution. We wish to start your
enterprise off on the right foot, so to speak, and the ladies of
the town have prepared something for you. Allow me to
introduce to you the widow of one of our most valiant
defenders of Vicksburg, who lost his life --

MRS. PEMBERTON
Mayor Washburn, there's no need to introduce me, either to
the citizens of Vicksburg, who know me well, or to Sergeant
Bates, considering that I descended on him yesterday
morning and spent the better part of an hour taking his
measurements. You may rest assured that the scene was one
of complete propriety, as I was assisted by Mrs. Partridge
and Mrs. Parker. Consequently, Sergeant Bates can hardly
be ignorant of what he is about to receive – unless he is more

thick-headed than most ... you expected me to say "Yankees", didn't you. No, although that word was on the tip of my tongue for four years straight, I've learned my lesson, as we all have. What I was about to say, and will say, is that he can hardly be ignorant of what he is about to receive unless he is more thick-headed than most soldiers. *[Laughter.]* Sergeant, the ladies of Vicksburg and indeed the ladies all along your intended route throughout the South would be mortified to have you endure your journey in such uncomfortable and, I dare say, disreputable, clothes as you have on. You and your flag and your mission deserve better. Therefore ...

[She looks over and a woman brings over the suit covered by a cloth.]

MRS. PARTRIDGE
We beg you to accept this as an expression of the admiration and appreciation of a grateful people.

[The cloth is removed to reveal a velvet walking suit. Its elegance may be incongruous, but it should in no way look laughable.]

BATES
Thank you.

MRS. PEMBERTON
I insist that you retire into the hotel and make the change immediately, first, so that we can be sure everything fits properly, second, so that the crowd can appreciate our handiwork, and third, because it does pain me to see you in those common clothes.

[Bates goes offstage with the walking suit. The crowd begins to mill around and to talk in small groups.]

FIRST MAN OR WOMAN IN CROWD

125

I must have missed something. Why are we honoring this Yankee?

[Pause.]

SECOND MAN OR WOMAN IN CROWD
I don't know. Because he's on our side?

FIRST
If so, why's he flauntin' the Union flag.

SECOND
Good question.

THIRD MAN OR WOMAN IN CROWD
He says there should be no more sides, no North and no South.

FIRST and SECOND
No more sides!!

FIRST
He doesn't understand Southern pride!

SECOND
Southern honor!

FIRST
There'll always be a South. We may have lost our army, but we'll never capitulate!

SECOND
They'll never force us to celebrate the Union victory! *[The last word is spat out.]*

FIRST
Or the Fourth of July!

SECOND
Or Lincoln's birthday!

FIRST
Or Washington's birthday!

THIRD
Washington was a Virginian.

SECOND
Then we'll celebrate it on a different day from the North!

[insert more from the unrepentant Rebels?]

MAYOR
Mabel, you've done a wonderful job. We all owe you a debt
of gratitude.

MRS. PEMBERTON
What, again? How many does that make. You must owe me
the keys to the city, your office, and the city treasury by
now. Just exactly when do you plan to pay off any of this
debt.

MAYOR
Uh, ...

MRS. PEMBERTON
I think we need to discuss this over a home-cooked meal.
Now I know you eat almost every evening at the Prentiss
House and I have no complaint about the food there, but
what about -- Sergeant!

*[Bates returns wearing the walking suit and carrying a
bundle of clothes.]*

BATES
It fits like a wonder. Thank you. Your generosity is ...

127

MRS. PEMBERTON
I'm so pleased it fits and you like it. I truly hope that every mile you walk is made a little easier and more comfortable through our simple efforts.

HOWARD
If you'd entrust your old clothes to me, Sergeant, I'll have them shipped home for you, along with an account for your family of this auspicious start to your march.

BATES
Well, thank you.

[Bates hands Howard the bundle of clothes.]

MAYOR
This is indeed an auspicious start and as you begin your journey ... Why are you looking at me like that. Oh, I almost forgot.

MRS. PEMBERTON
Sergeant, our Mayor is a wonderful man. He is a pillar of the community and he has many virtues, but I cannot list as chief among them his memory. I wasn't finished.

MAYOR
Mabel, I'm sorry.

MRS. PEMBERTON
We'll discuss your penance on another occasion. Sergeant, we measured you yesterday, and then we measured you again, the second time without tape. We three women who were there with you gained a deeper appreciation for your mission and your reverence for the flag and your love of this country, all of it. We also saw that you consider Reconstruction to be both unnecessary and demeaning to the people of the South. Inspired by what you gave us, we

128

resolved to contribute one more item to your cause.

[She looks over and a second woman brings the flag covered by a cloth.]

MRS. PARKER
We ask that you accept this, *[The flag is uncovered.]* and carry it on your journey. It was made by hands that five years ago stitched a different style of flag, but which this time felt the weighty responsibility of transferring that loyalty to the Stars and Stripes.

MRS. PEMBERTON
Your regimental flag, Sergeant, is far too precious to brave the elements again. It's earned its rest and its place of honor. Your regimental flag is also out-of-date, reflecting what was then, not what is now. Instead of thirty-six, there are now thirty-seven states and, as you know, every one of those stars is precious.

HOWARD
I can send your flag home with your clothes.

BATES
Ladies, you overwhelm me. Your thoughtfulness is ... I accept the gift, and also your offer, Mr. Howard.

[The flags are exchanged.]

MAYOR
Would you care to address the crowd, Sergeant?

BATES *[very awkward and clearly uncomfortable]*
I'm ... I'm not ... I'm not much for makin' speeches. I mostly want to get started. But since so many people came to see me and to honor the flag, I guess I owe it to you to say somethin', however poor. Citizens and ... friends. As you know, I intend to carry this flag across the South. Years

129

ago you arrayed yourselves in war against it, and it was an emblem of death and ruin to you. I carry it now as an emblem of peace and friendship and good will, and your response to it shows that defeat has been accepted with nobility and sincerity, and that union is once again possible. *[Cheers.]* Mrs. Partridge and the other women have done well to provide me with a flag that represents the country as it is now, not as it was then. Let "then" be forgotten – no, not forgotten, there are too many dear memories mixed in with the terrible memories of that time – not forgotten, but lamented and accepted and left behind. It's time to move on. And now it's time for me to move on.

SOMEONE IN THE CROWD
Three cheers for Sergeant Bates and the United States flag! Hip, hip ...

ALL BUT THE COMPLAINERS IN THE CROWD
hooray! Hip, hip, hooray! Hip, hip, hooray!

[The cheers continue. People reach out to touch Bates and to shake his hand. As he reaches the exit, he turns and waves the flag, causing an especially loud cheer. He exits. Lights down.]

==

==

Scene 8. Sending the News Home, Part I
The same set as Scene 2
February, 1868

[Ann E. and Hattie enter. They are both carrying shopping baskets, and Ann E. is carrying a wrapped package.]

ANN E.
Did we get everything?

HATTIE
Yes, Mama.

ANN E.
Is your basket too heavy?

HATTIE
No, Mama. What's in the package.

ANN E.
I don't know, but it came from Vicksburg. It must be from your father. Shall we open it right now?

HATTIE
Yes!

ANN E.
All right. I don't want to wait 'til we get home, either. Let's sit down. *[They sit and Ann E. partially opens the package.]* It's your father's clothes and his flag. He can't be .... *[She looks farther.]* Here's a note. "Dear Missus Bates, I have the honor of mailing to you Sergeant Bates's clothes and regimental flag, which he entrusted to me to send to you." He's all right. "He arrived in Vicksburg the day before yesterday, January 23rd, and today he was given a regal reception by the mayor and other prominent citizens before

131

he began his march, wearing a new walking suit and carrying a new banner, both sewn for him by the ladies of Vicksburg. By the time you receive this he will be well on his way across Mississippi. He sends you his best wishes and I am certain his undertaking will be successful. Yours respectfully, Mister Frank Howard. Vicksburg, Mississippi, January 25, 1868." Your father's all right, Hattie.

HATTIE
Did he write anything?

ANN E.
No, it appears he didn't.

HATTIE
When will he come home.

ANN E.
Not for awhile yet.

HATTIE
Will he be home before the kittens are grown up?

ANN E.
Yes. Yes, he will. Now let's go home. Do you remember where we tethered Chestnut?

HATTIE
Yes, Mama. May I give him the sugar?

ANN E.
Yes, go ahead.

[Hattie runs off, and Ann E. follows.]

End of Act I

===

Curtain Music to Act II

[As with the earlier curtain music, encourage the audience to sing.]

When Johnny Comes Marching Home
When Johnny comes marching home again, hurrah! hurrah!
We'll give him a hearty welcome then, hurrah! hurrah!
The men will cheer, the boys will shout, the ladies they will all turn out,
And we'll all feel gay when Johnny comes marching home.

Black is the Color
Black, black, black is the color of my true love's hair;
Her lips are something wondrous fair;
The bluest eyes and the daintiest hands;
I love the grass on which she stands.

===

Act II

Scene 9. On the Road
A country road.
February, 1868

[The sound of a cold wind. A rustic sign reads "flag train to stop". A man enters carrying a bag, wearing an overcoat, and huddled against the elements. He sets the bag down, moves a small red flag to a holder, and sits to rest. Bates enters, carrying the flag and obviously suffering from the cold. The man sees him and stands.]

MAN AT RAILROAD CROSSING
Howdy!

BATES
Hello.

MAN
You must be that sergeant. I heerd you might comin' through thisaway, but I never thought to see ya. *[Bates merely nods.]* I heerd about that fancy walkin' suit, too, but where's your coat.

BATES
I'm afraid I don't have one.

MAN
You must be frozen. It's cold enough to snow, 'n' we don' see that much here. Ain't ya cold?

BATES
Truth to tell, yes I am.

MAN

Well, take mine, then.

BATES
I couldn't. That would only trade my misery for yours.

MAN
If you're doin' what you said you set out to do -- 'n' I
waren't sure I believed you'd do it 'til I see you come round
that bend there – you'll be needin' it a peck more'n I will.

BATES
But you need it, too

MAN
Naw. I know how t' get along without one. There's been
times in winter when I've had a coat 'n' times when I
haven't. I was countin' myself lucky t' have one this year
but that's only 'cause the man who owned it ... didn't come
back from the fightin', 'n' I'd count myself even luckier t' be
able to give it t' you.

BATES
I really wouldn't feel right taking it.

MAN
Listen, are you cold?

[Beat.]

BATES
You bet I am.

MAN
All right, then. When the next train t' come down these
tracks stops t' pick me up, are you gonna get on it?

BATES
No, I'll keep walking.

MAN
That does it then. Here you go. *[He removes his overcoat and holds it out to Bates.]* Allow me to hold your flag while you put it on.

BATES
Thanks.

[The man takes the flag. Bates puts on the coat and takes back the flag.]

BATES
Thank you.

MAN
Well, you should find the road from here to Richmond a mite easier now, though it ain't a good time o' year t' be walkin' these roads at all. If the weather continues like this, you'll be in mud all the way, except when it's frozen.

BATES
How about the railroad beds. They'd be better, wouldn't they.

MAN
I reckon so. I walk the track when I go to Bovina, and once you get the right stride down, it's easy walkin'.

[A train whistle sounds, followed by the sound of a (small) steam engine slowing to a stop. The man removes the red flag from the holder and places it where it was before, and then picks up his bag in his left hand. He salutes the flag and shakes Bates's hand.]

MAN
Good-bye, Sergeant. Good luck.

[The man turns and leaves. Sounds of the train starting and leaving. Bates watches and walks off toward the tracks. Just as he exits ...]

A WOMAN'S VOICE FROM OFFSTAGE
Is that the man with the flag? Oh stop! I have to get off to greet him!

[Other offstage voices join hers. Sound of the train stopping again, then fade out.]

===

===

Scene 10. Southern Hospitality
The veranda of a Southern plantation home.
Early spring, 1868

[Bates is sitting with an elderly couple.]

BATES
Mrs. Ward, I've never had a better dinner. How can I thank
you for your hospitality.

MRS. WARD
I'm afraid it was very poor fare. If you could've been here
... in the old days.

MR. WARD
It's so hard to find anyone, white or black, who's willing to
work for a normal wage now.

MRS. WARD
I hope you'll stay with us more than just one night.

BATES
Enjoyable as that would be, I still have a long journey ahead
of me, another month at least. What's more, I'm
unfortunately no longer even master of my own time.

MRS. WARD
Why is that.

BATES
I find that the newspapers have been publicizing my route
and without consulting me they've been estimating my
arrival in various towns. When I arrived at Jackson I
discovered a large portion of the town had been awaiting my
arrival since early in the morning, as published, and by the
time I finally got there, many of them had gone home in

disappointment. So I find I have to walk faster and longer and harder than I would on my own, in order not to disappoint the readers of the newspapers.

MRS. WARD
But that's not fair to you.

BATES
Perhaps not, but "fair to me" isn't paramount. It's worth every step. Everywhere I go I'm received with kindness. There are speeches in my honor and in support of the flag. I could ask for no more. The generosity has been remarkable. One man even insisted -- on a day when I was truly suffering from the cold -- that I take the winter coat off his back. I'm overwhelmed by the willingness of those who have little to share or part with what they have, for someone in need. But I've found I must draw the line at money.

MR. WARD
Why. What happened.

BATES
Very early in my march, just as I started walking along the railroad tracks because the roads were so muddy and poor, a train stopped. All the passengers got out and made a fuss over me, and before I was prepared to handle the situation, a number of people forced money onto me, putting it into my pockets, a total of fourteen dollars. I know it was motivated by nothing but generosity, but it made me uncomfortable in the extreme.

MR. WARD
What did you do.

BATES
Being unable to return it to its rightful owners, I put it in an envelope and mailed it home. I'm certain my wife can put it to good use.

139

MRS. WARD
Your wife is able to manage without you?

BATES
Yes, she is. She's a very capable woman, better at some
things, like finances, than I am. I didn't want to leave her
with all the burdens of the farm, but ... I had to, and she let
me go.

MRS. WARD
Do you and your wife have any children?

BATES
A daughter, [five] years old.

MRS. WARD
Do you write to them?

BATES
I'm not much for writin'.

MRS. WARD
I'm sure I would have fallen completely to pieces if Mr.
Ward had left me. Luckily –

MR. WARD
Luckily, I was too old.

MRS. WARD
We're both still very fortunate, despite everything. I'm sure
your wife appreciates the kind of man you are to do this.

MR. WARD
And I'm sure you appreciate the kind of woman she is, to let
you go. *[Long pause.]* You're pensive. I apologize if we
made you miss your wife and family too much.

BATES
No.

MRS. WARD
It's human nature to care about one's family almost more
than about one's self.

[Pause.]

MR. WARD
Well, I hope you run across nothing more unpleasant in your
march than having money forced on you.

BATES
Thank you. That reminds me, though. I did have a very
disagreeable encounter a few days ago, and for the first time
– I hope the only time – I wished I'd had a weapon.

MRS. WARD
Oh no!

MR. WARD
But you escaped, and you're all right?

BATES
I did. I am. And now I can tell the story with an easy heart.
[He stands, picks up the furled flag, and acts out the story.]
A few miles west of Milledgeville, five curs, of a
disagreeable size --

MR.WARD
Are you referring to dogs or men?

BATES
Dogs, just dogs, sir. Well, they set upon me furiously, and
seemed determined to punish my intrusion. If it hadn't been
for my glorious flag-staff, I might not have survived to tell
the tale. The battle was hot and heavy for about fifteen

141

minutes. I plied the flag-staff with vigor and dexterity, and, at last, victory was mine.

MRS. WARD
Hurrah!

MR. WARD
Hurrah for the flagstaff!

BATES
I have thought about the incident over and over, and I'm afraid I can account for the hostility of the dogs only on the ground that they are rebels yet and have not been reconstructed. When I reach Washington, I intend to report the incident to the President and the Congress. It seems to me that such a display of rebellion will necessitate extending the military government over this unrepentant country.
[Bates sets the flag back and sits. Mr. and Mrs. Ward clap.]
Thank you. Telling you that story made me feel ... lighter than I have in a long time.

MR. WARD
No. Thank you. It does us good to hear a Northerner talk like that. You understand our plight. You see the unhappy condition of our country. You appreciate the necessity of forgetting and forgiving the past.

BATES
I do.

MR. WARD
The North defeated the South, as I suppose it had to, but it refuses to help us rebuild. I'm not talking about rebuilding this, though the destruction here was wanton: beautiful furniture, grand pianos, all destroyed.

MRS. WARD
What harm can a piano do.

MR. WARD
You've seen the cities and the countryside, Sergeant: vacant
houses everywhere, deserted warehouses, disintegrating
wharves, streets grown wild with grass, gardens choked with
weeds, desolate ruins, and acres of emptiness.

BATES
I've seen all that.

[Mr. Ward stands at some point during the following.]

MR. WARD
The Radicals in Washington treat us hatefully, seek to
degrade us, and do us great wrong. They set up a military
government over us, they took away the right of hundreds of
thousands of white men to vote, and they gave the Negroes
the ballot with no education whatever in civil government.
They are easily led astray and are now subject to the basest
influences. I truly hope for a restoration of the union, for the
longer this continues, the more resentment will grow. I fear
the enmity of reconstruction even more than I fear the
enmity of defeat.

MRS. WARD
Now, Mister Ward, sit down.

[Mr. Ward sits.]

BATES
I hear the same sentiments everywhere. Tell me, what's the
news from Washington. Has the Congress impeached
Johnson?

MRS. WARD
Yes. The House voted to impeach him, and now there'll be
a trial in the Senate.

143

BATES

What folly. President Johnson is a weak man, a foolish man, and he suffers immeasurably by comparison to his predecessor, but he is trying to carry out some of Lincoln's policies. If the Senate succeeds in removing Johnson from office, I fear even worse times for the South. I'd like to think that in some small way my effort might stem the tide of the Radicals' hatred and vindictiveness.

MRS. WARD

It will. It must.

BATES

Well, Mrs. Ward, Mr. Ward, I wonder if you would excuse me. I must be up and on my way early tomorrow.

MRS. WARD

Why of course. Now I see you're traveling light. You may not even be carrying writing paper. I keep thinking of your wife waiting back home for word from you. I'd be pleased to provide you with writing material or help you write a letter.

BATES

Do you really think I ought to?

MRS. WARD

She's starving for news!

BATES

But the newspapers are reporting my progress, and I sent a couple of telegrams.

MRS. WARD

Sergeant! Is reading about you in the paper the same as hearing from you?! I dare say not. She deserves better. Now what can I do to facilitate a letter home.

BATES

Well ... Listen. Do you hear something?

MRS. WARD
No.

MR. WARD
No, nothing. What do you hear.

[Pause. Bates is listening intently.]

BATES
Men. A large group of men. Did you invite guests?

MR. & MRS. WARD *[together]*
No.

[An indistinct sound of voices is heard. This is drawn out as long as possible. Bates stands and takes the flag again.]

MR. WARD
Who comes there!

GEORGE SANDERS
You got that Northern boy there? Well, hand him over, 'cause we plan to make him dance!

MR. WARD
George, is that you? What are you doing?

[George Sanders enters. His intentions for the next few lines should be ambiguous. Others begin to enter.]

GEORGE
This here Northern boy needs to be taught somethin' about the South.

MR. WARD
Now George --

GEORGE
Mister Ward. Sir. You always had the finest home in the
county and whatever you'd say, the people did it. But
tonight, it's our turn 'n' we're callin' the tune. This Northern
boy don't belong t' you.

*[One of last to enter carries a keg, and a couple carry
fiddles. They have already started drinking, most noticeably
George. During the next few lines they set up the keg and
tune up the fiddles.]*

GEORGE
He's goin' to be the principal guest for a little celebration.
We don't have much to celebrate around here nowadays. Is
this the renowned Sergeant Gilbert Bates of the First
Wisconsin Heavy Artillery?

[George salutes Bates, and Bates returns the salute.]

BATES
And whom do I have the honor of addressing?

GEORGE
Private George Sanders of the [Tenth Georgia Mountain
Volunteers].

BATES
You know, my friends in Wisconsin would never believe I'm
here, alive, in Georgia.

GEORGE
That's a insult 'n' a defamation! Sergeant, give me your
hand. I say, Sergeant, I was a rebel once, and I fought you
Northerners like hell; but we lost, 'n' we handed in our
checks; yes, sir, we quit, 'n' we intend to stay quit. That old
flag is all right now, and I for one am willing to fight for it
against anybody, and I can lick hell out of any man that dare

146

insult it, or you either, Sergeant. Isn't that so?

BATES
I'm sure it's so, but no more talk of fighting. We're soldiers of a common land now. You brought fiddles rather than field-pieces [music rather than muskets].

GEORGE
That's right. We brought fiddles and strong drink. You'll join us?

BATES
Mr. Ward, Mrs. Ward, this is your home. Do you approve?

MR. WARD
By all means.

BATES
Then I will. I may be moderate in my drinking, as I must be up and off early tomorrow, but I'll join you.

[Someone hands Bates a cup.]

[expand: a tale or two of camp life]

GEORGE
Say, do you know "Hard Times"?

BATES
Yes, I do. It's a beautiful song, and all too true.

GEORGE
Well, see if you recognize this. We used to sing it in camp when the victuals were a mite lean.

[The fiddles start playing "Hard Times" ("Hard Crackers") and some of the men sing.]

147

ONE OR MORE SOLDIERS
Let us close our game of poker, take our tin cups in hand,
While we gather around the cook's tent door.
Where dry mummies of hard crackers are given to each man.
Oh! Hard crackers, come again no more.
'Tis the song, the sigh of the hungry:
"Hard crackers, hard crackers, come again no more!
Many days you have lingered upon our stomachs sore!
Oh! Hard crackers, come again no more!"

*[The fiddles move on to "The Yellow Rose of Texas", and
some of the men start dancing. Mr. and Mrs. Ward join
them. Lights down very slowly.]*

===

Scene 11. A Warning
Augusta, Georgia
March 14, 1868

[The song dies away and is replaced by the sounds of people departing, then the sounds of the night in the South (an owl, etc.). The night sounds die away and are replaced by the sounds of a small city street at night (people, horses, carts, etc.) Lights up dim. Bates and another man stroll on. Bates is carrying nothing. The man wears a coat that conceals a pistol.]

MAN
I'm glad you enjoyed the play.

BATES
I did. Thoroughly. Thank you again for taking me.

MAN
Our theater here in Augusta may not be as splendid as the one in the capital, but we were luckier than they were. It survived the war intact, and once again it's become a focus of our civic aspirations and our creative expressions.

BATES
I never went to the one in Stoughton back home, but if they have entertainments like that, I'll have to take my wife and daughter when I return.

MAN
Maybe they'll have a play about you there someday.

BATES
Not very likely --

[Peter Thomas, an African-American man, rushes on from

149

the opposite side of the stage.]

THOMAS
Mister Bates? Sergeant, sir.

BATES
Yes?

THOMAS
You aren't safe here, sir.

MAN
What are you saying.

THOMAS
There are men waiting for you.

BATES
Armed?

THOMAS
They mean to shoot you.

MAN
White men?

THOMAS
No sir. Negroes. Put up to it by white men, though.

MAN
Who.

THOMAS
I'd rather not say. I'm taking enough of a chance as it is.

MAN
I know the type. White men who pretend to be the negroes'
friends, then they incite them to some outrageous mischief

by telling them someone's trying to enslave them again.

BATES
They know better than that, don't they?

THOMAS
I'm afraid not. Every Southern state, except Tennessee,
made it a crime to educate any Negro. Can you imagine
what it would be like to have no education at all: no readin',
no writin', no 'rithmatic, no history, and most of all, no
civics. No knowledge of how government works, except
what you hear from somebody else. I know that feelin', 'n'
I've been workin' to overcome it, but there's a lot to learn.

MAN
He's right. The responsibility for their ignorance does not lie
with the Negro, but giving them the vote with no preparation
whatsoever, was sheer folly. As a result, they -- and we --
are at the mercy of unscrupulous demagogues.

BATES
Why did you come to warn me.

THOMAS
Because we're brothers in blue.

BATES
I beg your pardon? You fought for the North?

THOMAS
Not just the North. Your own state.

BATES
You're from Wisconsin?

THOMAS
No. Actually, I'm from here, but after I ran away from my
master, who took me to war with him to help with the

151

baggage train, I joined the Twenty-first Wisconsin Infantry as a private. I'm very proud o' that. I came back here after the war, to find what was left of my family, and to better the Negroes' lot. I could tell you about that, but it's past time for me to leave.

BATES
Then thank you.

THOMAS
Yes sir. I'll be going.

MAN
Yes, thank you. Those white men're worse than the anthrax when it gets in a herd o' cattle.

[Thomas starts to leave in the direction from which Bates entered.]

BATES
Wait. What's your name.

THOMAS
If you don't mind, Sergeant, I'd rather not say that, either.

BATES
Why not. I'd like to know whom I have to thank, maybe for my life.

THOMAS
I don't need any more thanks.

MAN
He's right. He's put his life in danger by warning you.

BATES
From his own people?

MAN
No, from the Whites.

BATES
[To Thomas.] Is that so?

[Long pause.]

THOMAS
Sergeant, you marched through the town earlier today. And
you passed through the town square. Do you remember
that?

BATES
Yes, I do.

THOMAS
I was there watching you. I wasn't wearing my uniform,
though. Do you remember the town square?

BATES
Yes. A noble-looking old courthouse, flying an American
flag, I noticed. Perfectly sculptured hedges, inviting benches
to sit on, and some beautiful magnolias just beginning to
bloom. I didn't know their name 'til I asked someone. What
a rich and heady perfume they bestowed.

THOMAS
And from the tallest, oldest magnolia tree in the square, two
months ago hung one of my cousins. *[Beat.]* Good luck,
Sergeant, and good-bye.

[Thomas turns and leaves.]

BATES
Good bye. And thank you.

MAN

And good luck.

[Pause while Bates and the Man look at each other.]

BATES
You know the negroes, and the whites, around here better than I do. What do you recommend.

MAN
Yes, I know 'em. *[He opens his coat so his pistol is prominently visible.]* Just follow me. You'll arrive at your hotel safely.

[The man crosses the stage and exits, followed by Bates. Lights down.]

===

======================================

Scene 12. Bringing the News Home, Part II
The same set as Scene 2
Spring 1868

[Ann E. and Hattie enter, both carrying shopping baskets. If a well-behaved small cat is available, Hattie can hold it partly in and partly out of her basket. If a door is available, Bill comes out of the general store; otherwise, he can be onstage.]

BILL
Missus Bates, Hattie.

ANN E.
Oh hello, Mister Carter. How are you.

HATTIE
Hello, Mister Carter.

BILL
How are you, Hattie.

HATTIE
I'm fine. Do you want to see my favorite kitten.

BILL
I sure do. *[Either Hattie takes the cat out of her basket or Bill looks in it.]*
What's its name.

HATTIE
Mama told me to call it "Union", but its real name is "Tiger".

BILL
Well, I guess I like both of those names. And you, Missus Bates? How are you?

155

ANN E.
Well, all things considered, I'm fine, too. I just got a
telegram and a letter from Mister Bates. I haven't even
opened the letter yet. In the telegram he says he's in North
Carolina now. He's all right, and he sends his love to Hattie
and me. He also says to tell you and Mister Sorenson -- is he
in your store?

BILL
No.

ANN E.
Well, I'll go over to his shop, but if I don't find him, please
be sure to pass this on to him.

BILL
I will.

ANN E.
Mister Bates says to tell John and Bill "I left South Carolina
on my own two feet." Do you know what that means?

BILL
Uh, yes ma'am, I do.

ANN E.
Was that part of the wager?

BILL
No, well, not directly, but ...

[Long pause.]

ANN E.
Hattie, would you like to go on to the wagon and give
Chestnut some sugar?

156

HATTIE
Okay. Bye.

[Hattie runs off.]

ANN E.
Now can you tell me?

BILL
Well, I told him if he ever set foot in South Carolina with the flag, he'd ...

ANN E.
Yes?

BILL
He'd never come out again, unless it was in a coffin. Missus Bates, I feel real bad about Gilbert leavin' you ... again.

ANN E.
Well, I don't know how much of it was your fault or Mister Sorenson's. He seemed determined to do it.

BILL
He certainly was. Did you try to stop him?

[Pause.]

ANN E.
Not really. I know when his mind's made up. Did you?

[Beat.]

BILL
Yes. Yes, I did. I don't understand it. What he's doing is so foolhardy. It's as if he's trying to kill himself.

ANN E.

157

Men go off to change the world. Women change it every time a child is born.

BILL
Well, men can't do that. Maybe that's why they go off and do foolish things. He isn't melancholy at home, is he?

ANN E.
No, but I often don't know what he's thinking, and he doesn't talk a lot about some things. But the strange thing is, I feel like he's beginnin' to talk to me in his telegrams. I got his flag and his clothes, with a note from a Mister Howard, and then he, Mister Bates, sent me fourteen dollars that people gave him on the way, and he included a short note with it explainin' what it was for, 'n' ... then he started sendin' telegrams, 'n' even though he's thousands of miles away, I feel more ... included.

BILL
Sometimes a man needs a change to change, 'n' a sometime a man's sense of who he is expands, beyond himself, to his family, or his community or, sometimes when something like a war calls him, his country. I figure that's how our basic selfishness gets turned into somethin' called heroism or nobility or altruism.

ANN E.
Do you mind if I sit here? I think I'd like to open his letter and read it now, too.

BILL
Go right ahead.

[Ann E. sits.]

ANN E.
I wish you'd sit, too.

158

[Bill sits. She opens the letter and reads silently for a moment.]

ANN E.
I guess he must o' sent this a few days before he sent the telegram. It must've been just before he crossed into South Carolina. I think he took your words about the coffin seriously. He never wrote like this before. ... "Dearest. As you must know from accounts in the newspapers, my journey has been successful, more successful than I ever imagined, and I am welcomed everywhere I go. Some people have said what I am doing is brave or courageous. I wish I knew what those words really mean. Tomorrow I leave Georgia and set foot in South Carolina, the heart of secession. I am writing this to tell you why I am here and not with you, why I am not where you have every right to believe I belong, but even now I don't know how to explain it to you." *[Long pause.]* Mister Carter, I'm having trouble reading this ... but I want you to hear it, too. Would you mind reading it aloud?

BILL
Are you sure you want me to?

ANN E.
Yes, if you would, please.

[She hands the letter to Bill.]

BILL
Let's see. "... but even now I don't how to explain it to you. ... I embarked on this march to show our government in Washington how wrong it is to impose Reconstruction on the South, to prove to Northern doubters that Southern folk are ready to accept the outcome of the conflict and to rejoin the Union and get on with their lives, and to follow President Lincoln's words that you read to me: 'With malice toward none, with charity for all, let us strive on to finish the work

159

we are in, to bind up the nation's wounds, to care for him who shall have borne the battle and for his widow and his orphan.' I do not know if I will reach Washington or ever see you again. In the endless hours walking, my mind travels long distances. When I started, I thought mainly of the distance that lay between me and Washington. Now I think more and more of the distance between us, between me and you and Hattie and home. I hope to return to you. If I should not, think of me as having failed to return in body only, for my spirit knows now that its home is with you, always. If I should die here, I will still return to be with you, for my spirit has no greater desire. If I should die, I will look down upon you always from the night sky, and I will caress you in the warm breezes of summer. Give Hattie a kiss for me, and take one for yourself as well. Yours faithfully, Gilbert."

ANN E.
Thank you, Mister Carter. It's good I received both of these at the same time, and that I read the telegram first, or I don't know what I would've done. I think I'd better go home now.

BILL
The telegram is indeed good news. I'll tell John. We all hope for Gilbert's safe return. Good-bye.

ANN E.
Good-bye.

[Ann E. exits. Lights down.]

===

==

Scene 12. A Soldier's Soul
The same set as Scene 2
Spring, 1868

*[The wooden cross present in scene 2 is now more visilble.
Bates enters with Gabriel, who limps as before. Bates limps
at least as much. The soldier carries and sets down an axe.]*

GABRIEL
You sure your ankle's all right?

BATES
It'll be okay.

GABRIEL
It don't look okay.

BATES
Oh, it's swollen, but it'll get better. Were you really waiting
for me since yesterday?

GABRIEL
I occupied myself choppin' wood.

BATES
Did it mean that much to see me?

[Beat.]

GABRIEL
I wanted to see you. Sarah! Calvin! Milly!

*[Sarah, Calvin and Milly come running in from different
directions.]*

SARAH

161

Did you find him? Oh! Excuse me.

[Sarah primps hurriedly and then straightens the children, who look at Bates intently.]

GABRIEL
Sergeant, allow me to introduce to you my wife Sarah, my son Calvin, and my daughter Millicent. This is Sergeant Gilbert Bates.

SARAH
Pleased to meet you.

BATES
It's my pleasure. You have a fine-looking family. Your daughter especially reminds me of mine back home in Wisconsin. She's about the same age.

SARAH
Sergeant, can we ask you to stay with us this evening and share a simple meal?

BATES
I'm sorry, but I really can't stay. I have to reach Fayetteville by tomorrow afternoon.

SARAH
But that's a good day's walk!

BATES
All the more reason I can't stay.

GABRIEL
Why, if I may ask, must you be in Fayetteville tomorrow.

BATES
That's when the newspaper said I'd be there. The papers always seem to set the earliest possible time, so the people

162

won't miss me, but that means I have to get there on time or people are disappointed.

GABRIEL
I assure you I wouldn't've dragged you two miles out of your way just to meet my family. At least not my livin' family. My brother's buried over there, and we have some unfinished business. Now that you're here, we can put a couple o' things t' rest. Calvin, go get me that packet under my bed. *[Gabriel looks at Calvin and points toward the cabin. Calvin runs off.]* You know, for a long time I hated you Yankees. I felt you made me break a promise I made to my brother. I don't know what I'd'a' done if you'd'a' come by here two years ago. But now, Sergeant, it may strike you as strange, but you get to be the representative of the entire Grand Army of the Republic. I have something to return to you.

BATES
Return something? To me?

GABRIEL
I have another flag to give you.

[Calvin returns with a package containing a folded flag, which he hands to Gabriel.]

GABRIEL
This flag belonged to a corps headquarters. It cost General Rosser some hard fighting and a good many lives to capture it, but you've recaptured it without firing a gun. Take it; it's yours.

[Bates places his flag someplace and takes the other flag.]

BATES
I accept it, for the entire Grand Army of the Republic, in the spirit of peace and reconciliation.

163

GABRIEL
It's good to let things go home again. That's the way it should be.

BATES
When I was in Winsboro, I was called to the bedside of a Captain, once in the Confederate army. He was suffering from the effects of injuries received during the war, and he was very near his end. He had sent for me, as a Northern man, to express the thoughts which lay nearest his heart. He spoke of the war, and the desolation which it had wrought, of the passion and hatred which it had engendered, and the North's present policy of resentment and distrust. .... He thanked me for my efforts to dispel the false impressions prevailing in the minds of the Northern people, and hoped that I would be successful. ... I bade him good-bye in sadness, and the news of his death reached me soon after.

SARAH
You seem to carry a great weight on your shoulders, Sergeant, along with your flag.

BATES
My burdens are small, consisting of little more than separation from my family and long weary marches through rain and mud. Those are small things compared to the future of a nation.

GABRIEL
I had another, more personal, reason for bringin' you here. I hope you don't mind. I asked you to come here to ... to visit my brother's grave. *[Pause.]* It's over there. *[Bates places the second flag in his haversack, and they walk to a simple wooden cross.]* You see, we fought side by side at Cedar Mountain and at Manassas, the second battle o' Manassas. I was wounded there, but it was just a scratch on my leg 'n' I stayed in the ranks. Finally, as we were advancin' at Ox Hill,

164

he took a bullet in his chest. *[Long pause. His vision grows distant and misted.]* For just a second, I couldn't decide whether t' keep advancing or whether t' stop 'n help him. I haven't told this t' anyone else. I stopped. I put down my rifle, 'n' I held 'im. There was so much blood we both knew it wouldn't be long. He told me he didn't mind dying, so long as we were victorious in the end. I told him I was sure we would be, 'n' that I could see the Yankee lines breaking, which wasn't true. He told me to remember him after the war was over, 'n' t' love my family, 'n' I said I'd do the best I could. His last words were "Tell them I love all of 'em *[Beat.]* 'n' you, too." I wanted t' do somethin' for him, but I couldn't. When he died in my arms, he suddenly seemed so heavy. I laid him down, 'n' said a prayer, 'n' got up 'n' kept fightin'. That was the day we took that flag. At the end o' the day, I came back 'n' made sure he was buried proper in a proper wooden coffin, 'n' afterward I went back 'n' brought him home. He died still believing in the cause, and even though that's long over now, I ... I want him t' rest easy.

[They go to the grave and stand on opposite sides. There is a long silence.]

BATES
Would it be all right if we bring the flag over?

GABRIEL
Yes, sir. Sarah, bring over the Sergeant's flag.

[Sarah brings the flag and holds it at the head of the grave.]

GABRIEL
Sergeant, you don't know how a soldier feels who returns from a war without a victory parade in his honor, feelin' like he fought in vain.

BATES
I understand better than you think.

165

[After another long pause, Gabriel extends his hand to Bates, who clasps it for a long moment.]

GABRIEL
Thank you, Sergeant.

[They walk back. Sarah follows with the flag and returns it to where Bates left it.]

MILLY
Mama, may I?

SARAH
Yes, you may. *[Milly runs off.]* Sergeant, thank you for taking your valuable time to ease my husband's heart. It means a lot to all of us. At the risk of delaying you further, my daughter wants to ask you something, and I've said she could. Would you consider it improper of me to ask you something myself?

BATES
Not at all.

SARAH
Why are you doing this?

[Pause.]

BATES
Somebody should.

SARAH
That's not an answer. Excuse me for that. But, why you.

[Long pause.]

BATES

Because men like your husband's brother gave their all in the war. Both North and South. I went, too, but I came back without a scratch. In fact, I was stationed in Washington and ... I never saw action. I need to do something ... remotely like what your husband and his brother did.

GABRIEL
You have.

[Bates and Gabriel look at each other for a long moment. Milly comes running back in, carrying a simple cornhusk doll. She looks at Sarah, who nods "yes". Milly stands upright and attempts a salute. Bates gets down on his knees before her.]

BATES
Your name is Milly?

MILLY
Yes ... sir.

BATES
Just "yes" is fine, and you don't have to salute. Now what did you want to ask me.

MILLY
You said you have a little girl back home.

BATES
Yes I do. Her name's Hattie.

MILLY
Does she like dolls?

BATES
Uh, yes, I guess she does.

167

MILLY

This is my favorite doll. Mama made her for me. I wouldn't trade her for anything, but I want to give it to you to give to Hattie.

[Bates, overcome by emotion, hugs Milly, then takes the doll reverently, kisses Milly on the forehead, and stands up. Lights down.]

==

==

Scene 13. Homeward Bound
On a train from Washington to Wisconsin.
Late April or early May, 1868

[The sound of a moving train. The stage is dimly lit. A few seats represent a railroad carriage. Arthur Colfax is seated in a pool of light, writing. Bates enters and walks past him.]

COLFAX
Sergeant!

[Bates stops and turns around.]

BATES
Mister ... Colfax, the reporter. Right?

COLFAX
Yes.

BATES
You know, I've met so many people on this trip. I'm a little surprised I remember your name, but then I did see the article you wrote about me. It wasn't very flattering.

COLFAX
No.

BATES
You wrote something about my limping into Washington with black eyes and one leg and one eye and one arm.

COLFAX
Well, I think you deserved that. You were a damn fool to do what you did. I'm not sure I completely understand your success, but ...

BATES
But I dare say I proved you wrong in the end.

COLFAX
I'm prepared to admit defeat. You indeed proved my
predictions wrong.

BATES
Doesn't a wrong prediction affect the success of your
column?

COLFAX
I figure the newspaper business is like a poker game. If I'm
right more often than I'm wrong, I win. And to tell the truth,
I could be wrong all the time as long as people read my
articles and like 'em. I don't have to be right, I just have to
be entertaining. So give me something to write about, to be
right about. Or better yet, tell me another fantastic story.
Tell me you're going to carry the flag across Canada, or
England, for no reason at all.

BATES
Perhaps I'd better move on to another seat.

COLFAX
No, sit down.

[Colfax motions at the seat across from him.]

BATES
I don't think so. I learned a lesson from travelin' with you
before.

COLFAX
No, you're safe. I promise to behave, as well as I can.
You've impressed me, and that changes things. *[Bates sits.]*
I see you're still carrying that flag. Doesn't it ever leave
you?

BATES
No, We're inseparable, at least 'til I get home. But this isn't
actually the flag you saw me carrying four months ago.

COLFAX
Oh, that's right. I read about you in Vicksburg. New flag.
New walking suit. Is that what you're wearing now?

BATES
A little the worse for wear. You know, I rode this train once
before, coming home from Washington after mustering out
in June of sixty-five. That time I rode in a car just like this
and I sat up late talking with Corporal Cooper. I can't
remember his first name now, just Corporal Cooper.

COLFAX
Another Wisconsin man?

[Bates nods.]

BATES
He died a while ago, just as I was startin' this trip. I
remember it as if it were yesterday, the train ride, I mean.
Did you know the Iron Brigade -- Wisconsin men mostly --
had the greatest combat losses in the entire Union army?
Especially at Antietam. He was at Antietam. I can still hear
him talkin' about it: "I fought and fell in fell Antietam's
fields, that day that robbed more mothers of their sons than
any else, in four war years." He had a way of expressing
himself, of making you see what he saw: "so this is it: here's
death, here's war; now be a man like all the rest, and kill."
"The military victory was slight, the only fruit of twenty
thousand deaths, the only crop that grew in barren fields
watered by the blood of fallen men: emancipation. Lincoln
freed the slaves, and we who fell were freedom's sacrifice."
Listening to him made me feel ... little, and I felt sorry to be
goin' home without having seen action.

COLFAX
Don't tell me you wanted to die.

BATES
It isn't that. *[Beat.]* I wouldn't try to make you understand.
You only see the worst motive behind everything.

COLFAX
That's the professional outlook of the skeptic. Never accept
the official line. Why, I even see Secretary of War Stanton
behind Lincoln's assassination. But I promise not to laugh or
ridicule. What was it you wanted.

BATES
Since I didn't take an active part in the war, I needed to
contribute something that could stand alongside the
sacrifices made by others. And what was most needed at
this time was to bind up the nation's wounds. I did what I
could. Whether I was successful or not, I may never really
know.

[Long pause.]

COLFAX
I understand. And that's what led you here?

BATES
Yes. Yes, it was.

COLFAX
You've had quite an adventure. I heard you made it to
Washington safely -- no missing limbs and nary a black eye -
- but you did have a little trouble there.

BATES
You might say that.

COLFAX
Tell me about it.

BATES
Surely you already know all about it.

COLFAX
I'm a reporter. That means I know better than to believe
what I read in the paper. I want to hear you tell it.

BATES
Well, when I arrived in Washington I was greeted by my
own senator, Senator Doolittle. He went with me to the
Capitol Building, to end a fourteen-hundred mile march by
flying the flag there. We stopped in on the way at the White
House 'n' we were received by President Johnson, who
thanked me for my efforts. When we got to the Capitol, the
officer there said the Senator could enter, but he had orders
not to admit me. There was nothing for us to do but leave.
The Senator did seem mighty upset, and he eventually took
me to the Washington Monument, where I gave my last
speech and flew my flag for the last time. So the only place
in this great country, North or South, where my message of
reconciliation was unwelcome was at the U.S. Capitol.

COLFAX
You certainly made the Radicals show their true colors.
Your reception, or rather your rejection, at the Capitol sent
as strong a message as your successful odyssey across the
South.

BATES
Is there any news from Washington?

COLFAX
The Senate voted. Didn't you hear?

BATES

No! What did they do.

COLFAX
They acquitted the president. By one vote.

BATES
And Doolittle! How did he vote!

COLFAX
For acquittal. He and just eighteen others. He broke ranks
with his party, and there's no chance he'll be returned to the
Senate when his term is up. That was his sacrifice. *[Pause.]*
Sergeant, you did that.

BATES
No. No, I don't think so. But all the same ...

[He smiles, mostly inwardly. Lights down.]
===

==

Scene 14. The End of the Journey
The same set as Scene 2.
Late April or early May, 1868.

[A crowd of well-wishers is waiting for Bates. Adults, some of whom carry band instruments, are talking. Children are playing. A large sign reads "Welcome home, Sergeant Bates." A train whistle is heard, followed by the sound of a train slowing and stopping. Ann E. and Hattie exit and the crowd edges closer to the depot. The band starts playing "Marching Through Georgia", the first verse and the refrain, with one or more vocalists.]

ONE OR MORE VOICES
Bring the good old bugle, boys, we'll sing another song --
Sing it with a spirit that will start the world along --
Sing it as we used to sing it, fifty thousand strong,
While we were marching through Georgia.

"Hurrah, hurrah, we bring the jubilee!
Hurrah, hurrah, the flag that makes you free."
So we sang the chorus from Atlanta to the sea,
While we were marching through Georgia.

[Shortly after the train stops, Bates enters, carrying the flag and hand-in-hand with Hattie. Ann E. is a step behind, carrying the haversack. The crowd cheers.]

BILL
Three cheers for Sergeant Bates! Hip, hip –

ALL
Hooray!

BILL
Hip, hip –

ALL
Hooray!

BILL
Hip, hip –

ALL
Hooray!

[The band starts playing again, the last verse.]

ONE OR MORE VOICES
So we made a thoroughfare for Freedom and her train,
Sixty miles in latitude -- three hundred to the main;
Treason fled before us far, resistance was in vain --

BATES
Stop!

BILL
What's wrong. You were serenaded by hundreds of bands on
your march. You don't like your hometown one?

BATES
It's not that at all. No band ever sounded sweeter, especially
when I know all the faces in it. It's just the choice of music.
Not once on my march did I hear that tune.

BILL
Well, what could be more appropriate than "Marching
through Georgia"?

BATES
That song's about war and destruction, and division. If you
don't mind, I'd prefer "America". *[He looks at the band
leader, who nods and motions to the band members to
change their sheet music.]*

176

BATES
Hello, friends. Well John, what do you say now.

JOHN
I say ... I say ... I still can't believe those rebels are
reconstructed, but you proved me wrong, and there's no
question you won our bet, and I'm ready to pay up, a dollar
for every day you were on the road. One hundred dollars.

BATES
I was only on the road eighty-one days from Vicksburg to
Washington.

JOHN
I'm countin' the days from here to Vicksburg, and from
Washington back here. You were away from your farm for a
hundred days. I think you owe the whole amount to your
long-suffering wife.

BATES
But the wager was –

BILL
Gilbert, we all know how honest and scrupulous you are.
Don't worry. You aren't takin' any more'n you deserve.
Besides, your name's been in the paper every week, 'n' your
notoriety's given John 'n' me 'n' the other shopkeepers in
town many times a hundred dollars worth o' trade. You're
famous.

BATES
For a few weeks. I'll be forgotten soon enough. I just hope
my walk contributed something to a reconciliation among
the states.

A VOICE IN THE CROWD
Speech!

OTHER VOICES
Speech! Speech!

BATES
You don't want to hear a speech from me.

BILL
Why not. You gave scores of speeches on your march.

BATES
You all know me, and I know you. I can't give a speech to you. You'd all laugh.

A VOICE
You're famous! Come on. Speech!

BATES
No, I can't give a speech to you.

[General dissatisfaction.]

BATES
Well, I guess I could repeat one of the speeches I gave on the way.

[General approval.]

BATES
Well, as I guess you know from the newspaper reports, I was allowed to raise my flag over every city hall and county courthouse and state capitol building I visited.

BILL
All except Washington.

BATES
Except Washington. You read about that.

BILL
We sure did. What an insult to you and to the flag! That has to have soured a few people on the Radicals.

BATES
Well, they made me give a lot o' speeches, and I got a lot better at public speaking by the end of the trip. The next-to-last one was at Richmond, Virginia. It went more or less like this:

[The lights dim on the rest of the stage and a spotlight isolates Bates, who looks into the distance and addresses the audience.]

When I began my march, I never could have imagined the reception I have received across the South. And how could I possibly have imagined that near the end of that march, here in Richmond, I would be allowed to ascend to the dome of this statehouse, the building that was the capitol of the Confederate States of America, there to wave my flag over the city that was once the stronghold of the rebellion. I speak now to everyone in this chamber and to everyone I have met over the past two-and-a-half months across the South. For your demonstrations of friendship for me, and respect for the flag of our country, I thank you. I am thus confirmed in my convictions respecting the sentiments of the Southern people. Heaven be praised that those convictions have proven correct. You will probably never see me again. I will pass from your sight, and from your thoughts, and be forgotten, but this flag will remain with you forever. It is your banner; it is your hope and pride as well as mine. I pray that before long it may wave over a happy and prosperous people, who entertain no ill will towards each other; that from its waving folds only blessings may descend upon the citizens of our country.

[The spot goes out as the lights onstage go back up. Bates

179

looks around, unsure for a moment of where he is. There is an awkward pause, then applause.]

Sorry. Where was I. Oh yes, in Richmond.

JOHN
Let's see that flag, that flag stitched by the hands of Southern rebel ladies.

BATES
John, I don't want to hear that word.

JOHN
Yes sir! Anything you say, sir. God, you're going to be insufferable from now on.

BATES
Just on this one point.

JOHN
All right, stitched by Southern belles. Is that better?

BATES
Yes. Stitched by ... Mrs. Pemberton and her friends. That seems a very long time ago.

[He unfurls and waves the flag. Cheers.]

BATES
This would be a good time for the band to play.

[The band plays "America", with one or more vocalists, and the crowd quickly joins in. Encourage the audience to sing by having the band play alone the first time through and then play it again?]

ONE OR MORE VOICES
My country, 'tis of thee,

Sweet land of liberty,
Of thee I sing.
Land where my fathers died,
Land of the Pilgrim's pride,
From ev'ry mountainside
Let Freedom ring.

BATES
I have one other important task. I have a small gift for a
very special small person. Hattie, come here. Ann E.,
would you bring me my haversack?

*[Ann E. gives him the haversack. As she does, he looks at
her fondly and does something affectionate, to which she
responds. Hattie goes slowly to Bates, cowed not by him but
by the crowd.]*

HATTIE
Yes, Papa?

[Bates kneels to get to her level.]

BATES
I have a present for you. You do like dolls, don't you?

HATTIE
Yes, Papa.

BATES
I met a very nice man on my journey, and he had a daughter,
a lot like you. And she had a favorite doll that her mother
made for her. And when she heard about you, she gave me
this to give to you.

*[He takes out the doll wrapped in a handkerchief, unwraps
it, and gives it to her.]*

HATTIE

It's made out of cornhusks. It's not as nice as my dolls.

[Bates is momentarily flustered. He looks at Ann E., who comes and puts her hand on his shoulder.]

ANN E.
But it's a very special doll.

BATES
It is. It means a lot to me. Promise me you'll take good care of it, and love it, for me.

HATTIE
Yes, Papa, I will, for you.

[Bates kisses Hattie as he kissed Milly. Curtain.]

End of Act II

The Historical Record.

Except for the reconstructed and invented dialogue, the rearrangement of events, and the other devices needed to bring this to the stage, this is a true story. Gilbert Bates served with the First Wisconsin Heavy Artillery from September 17, 1864 to June 26, 1865. After the war he wrote a 36-page pamphlet entitled "Triumphal March of Sergeant Bates from Vicksburg to Washington", completing it in "Albion, near Edgerton, June 20, 1868". It was published later the same year by Intelligence Printing House in Washington. A copy of the pamphlet can be found at the Wisconsin Historical Society.

The plight of African-Americans in the post-war South occupied very little of Gilbert Bates's attention. He made only a few references in his pamphlet to freed slaves or other African-Americans, mostly seeming to find that they were being led to believe that they would be provided for by the Reconstruction program, especially the Freedmen's Bureau, in ways that were illusory, such as the never-realized promise of "forty acres and a mule" apiece.

The crucial vote in the Senate following the impeachment of President Andrew Johnson was taken on May 16, 1868, a few weeks after Bates finished his march. The Northern Radical Senators failed by one vote to remove President Johnson from office. Senator Doolittle was one of the 19 senators who voted against removal. Doolittle was not in fact wavering at the time Bates met him, but other senators were, especially Edmund G. Ross of Kansas, whose story is one of the biographies in John F. Kennedy's Profiles in Courage.

Some of the phrases attributed to Arthur Colfax in scene 11 were actually written by Mark Twain. The following appeared in the <u>Territorial Enterprise</u> on February 27, 1868:

More Westonism.

Sergeant Gilbert H. Bates of Wisconsin is the last candidate for pedestrian notoriety. He has made a bet that he will walk, alone, unarmed, without a cent in his pocket, and bearing aloft the American flag, through the late Southern Confederacy, from Vicksburg to Washington. He is already on his way, and the telegraph is noting his progress. The Mayor and a large portion of the population of Vicksburg ushered him out of that city with a grand demonstration. He proposes to sell photographs of himself at 25 cents apiece, all along his route, and convert the proceeds into a fund to be devoted to the aid and comfort of widows and orphans of soldiers who fought in the late war, irrespective of flag or politics. And then, I suppose, when he gets a good round sum together, for the widows and orphans, he will hang up his flag and go and have a champagne blow-out. I don't believe in people who collect money for benevolent purposes and don't charge for it. I don't have full confidence in people who walk a thousand miles for the benefit of widows and orphans and don't get a cent for it. I question the uprightness of people who peddle their own photographs, anyhow, whether they carry flags or not. In my opinion a man might as well start his name with an initial and spell his middle name out and hope to be virtuous.

But this fellow will get more black eyes, down there among those unconstructed rebels than he can ever carry along with him without breaking his back. I expect to see him coming into Washington some day on one leg and with one eye out and an arm gone. He won't amount to more than an interesting relic by the time he gets here and then he will have to hire out for a sign for the Anatomical Museum. Those fellows down there have no sentiment in them. They won't buy his picture. They will be more likely to take his scalp.

     Mark Twain
     Washington, January 30, 1868

Surrounded by Reality

commissioned by Historic Madison, Inc.
and written for The Madison Theatre Guild
by John Nicholas Schweitzer
4713 Regent Street
Madison, WI 53705
608-231-3941

Prologue
>Part 1 - in Forest Hill Cemetery
>Part 2 - in the living room and attic

Scene 1 - 1862: Camp Randall

Entr'acte 1

Scene 2 - 1883: the Collapse of the Capitol Wing

Entr'acte 2

>Intermission

Scene 3 – 1922: Greenbush

Entr'acte 3

Scene 4 - 1963: the Fair Housing Ordinance

Epilogue

Forest Hill Cemetery, Madison, 2006

Cast: Guide
Edwin, African-American male, about 50
Sarah, Caucasian female, about 50
Martin, mixed race, about 20
Holly, mixed race, about 15
others, with lines for 2 to 6

*The guide leads a group of people onstage in front
of the curtain. Consider having some or all of them
carry umbrellas in the cemetery as a reference to
"Our Town".*
*Included in the group are Edwin and Sarah, (older
versions of the couple we meet in scene 4), their son
Martin, and their daughter Holly. The costumes,
mostly contemporary t-shirts, shorts and running
shoes, indicate the time as the present. [The logos
on the t-shirts should be topical or humorous, e.g.
MTG, HMI, Bring the Troops Home Now.]*
*Someone takes out a cell phone and makes a call as
soon as the Guide starts talking.*

GUIDE
Follow me. We'll start over here, where you'll be able to see
both the Confederate cemetery and some Indian mounds.

He stops and waits for the group to assemble.

CALLER
We're starting! Where are you! *Pause.* All right, just join
the group when you get here. [You can't miss us. We look
like a gaggle of umbrellas.]

GUIDE
Can everybody hear me? My name's Mark and I'll be your

189

guide for this Historic Madison tour of Forest Hill Cemetery.
Right now you're in one of the oldest sections, but we'll pass
through many different eras before we're done. Are there
any questions before I start?

MARTIN
Indian mounds?

GUIDE
You can actually see three from here. The most impressive
one is the effigy mound in the shape of a goose. You're
standing right next to it. The long neck stretches out to your
left and the two wings --

MARTIN
Cool! Indians built them, right?

> *While the Guide answers, Martin moves around to*
> *take a photo of the mound with a digital camera,*
> *then shows the result on the LCD viewer to Holly.*

GUIDE
The most accepted theory is that they were built by the
ancestors of the Winnebago, now known as the Ho-Chunk.
No place in the world enjoyed such a dense concentration of
mounds as Madison.

A VOICE
Do you suppose the Indians had their own tours of the
mounds?

GUIDE
I'm glad you asked that. I like to imagine they did. You
know, on July Fourth, 1837, when the cornerstone of the first
Capitol was laid, there was a big party in Madison, and a
band of Winnebago Indians joined the festivities, led by

Chief Little Dandy. I like to imagine he gave the new
settlers a tour of the mounds on the Isthmus. But even he
probably spoke of the mysterious ancestors who made them.

A VOICE
Who were the first settlers?

GUIDE
The first "white" people to actually settle in Madison were
Eben and Rosaline Peck. They built a small cabin about a
block from where the Capitol is now, that served as general
store and tavern and rooming house.

A VOICE
Did the Indians and the settlers get along?

GUIDE
The Native Americans who lived in this area treated the new
arrivals with tolerance. They had a tremendous reverence
for the land, but they didn't feel they "owned" it, and selling
plats of land, as James Doty did, was mysterious to them.

SARAH
I think my great-grandfather's buried here somewhere.

GUIDE
What was his name.

SARAH
David Atwood.

GUIDE
Oh yes, we'll see his grave right over there, and if you're a
descendant of Mister Atwood, we'll see some of your other
relatives before we're done.

SARAH

191

We're surrounded by the spirits of our ancestors here.

The Guide talks as he walks off. Everyone follows him.

GUIDE
Right over there is the northernmost Confederate cemetery in the United States. We'll come back to that at the end, but the first marker I want to point out is right over here, if you'll follow me. It's the grave of Darwin Clark, who arrived in Madison in June of 1837 with the first crew of workers to build the Capitol. He was certainly at that Fourth of July celebration, and it may well have been Darwin Clark who had too much to drink that day and shot Rosaline Peck's two pet crows. Anyway, Clark stayed in Madison for more than 50 years after that. *[offstage]* He became one of the growing town's leading businessmen, and he held many positions of distinction.

The Caller remains on stage as the Truant enters.

TRUANT
Kate!

CALLER
You're here!

TRUANT
Sorry. I got lost. You won't believe where I ended up!

CALLER
Well, come on!

TRUANT
Hey wait, look at this! "Michael Zwank, 1828-1883, stone mason killed in the Capitol collapse." I wonder what that means.

CALLER
Will you –

TRUANT
Or this one: "James John Adams Riley, known as
'Snowball'". What a name!

CALLER
Weird, but can we join the group?!

TRUANT
Sure.
    They exit, following the Guide.

193

PROLOGUE - Part 2
The living room of the Anderson house, 2006

*The curtains open or the lights come up on the living
room of the family's house, with furnishings that
identify the time as today. Edwin, Sarah, Martin
and Holly enter in the same clothes, and Holly is
listening to music.*

SARAH
Holly. Holly! Can you turn that music down? *[Holly puts
earphones in.]* Thank you. Are you sure you can't stay
home for the rest of the afternoon? We never get to see you
these days.

MARTIN
I'm on the phonebank this afternoon for Action Wisconsin.

EDWIN
Do you have to?

MARTIN
Yes! It's important! Do you know that those conservatives
are trying to ban civil unions!

EDWIN
I know. But do you have to spend all your time on that.
Don't you have any other interests?

MARTIN
I do, and I would, but society isn't giving me that choice.

SARAH
We know, dear. We don't want to keep you. Can you at
least stop by again after you're done?

MARTIN

194

I don't know. I'll see. Yeah, sure.

SARAH
All right. See you later.

MARTIN
Yeah. Bye, Mom. Bye, Dad. Holly. *She doesn't hear him.*
Holly, bye!

HOLLY
Are you leaving?

MARTIN
Yeah.

HOLLY
Wait. Are you coming to my birthday party?

MARTIN
Am I invited?

HOLLY
Yes, silly.

MARTIN
How about Greg.

HOLLY	EDWIN
Of course!	No!

MARTIN
Yeah, I knew it.

EDWIN
Don't act surprised. You know how I feel.

SARAH
Edwin, we want Martin here for Holly's sixteenth –

EDWIN
Martin's welcome by himself.

MARTIN
If Jack isn't welcome, then I'm not, either. We've been together for two years. By the time you guys were together two years you were engaged.

HOLLY
This is a disaster.

> *She puts her earphones back in and starts listening to her music again.*

MARTIN
I'm gone. Bye, Mom.

> *Martin leaves.*

EDWIN
I'm the head of this family, and –

SARAH
Never mind. He's gone. Let's just change the subject.

> *Long pause.*

SARAH
Holly? *Holly doesn't hear her. She raises her voice.* Holly!

HOLLY
What.

SARAH

Could you stop listening to your music for a minute?

HOLLY
Okay.

She removes her earphones.

SARAH
So what did you think of the cemetery tour?

HOLLY
It was okay.

EDWIN
Just okay? I bet you had some thoughts.

HOLLY
Yeah, Dad.

EDWIN
And?

HOLLY
Well, like, you know, it was kind of creepy to think of dead people in the ground there, right under your feet sometimes, but, you know, the stories, like, made them real.

SARAH
This may sound strange, but I had a wonderful time. It made me think of what I'll leave behind when I go. In fact, I realized that even though I spend a lot of my time and effort on my job and our finances, the most important answer to what I'll leave behind is -- *turning to Holly and hugging her* -- you and your brother, and that makes me happy. *To Edwin.* How did you like it, dear?

EDWIN

It was interesting and informative, but ... after we'd been there for awhile, it ... it bothered me.

SARAH
Bothered you? Why.

EDWIN
I mean, the tour was great, but I started thinking about our family, too, and it had the opposite effect on me. Family is the most important thing! And I love Holly, but ... how can Martin do that to us!

SARAH
What is he doing to us.

EDWIN
He's ... you know.

SARAH
What do you mean.

EDWIN
You know very well what I mean!

Holly puts her earphones back in.

SARAH
You're being unreasonable.

EDWIN
He has family responsibilities.

SARAH
What are you talking about.

EDWIN
If he doesn't get married and have children, it's the end of

the family name!

SARAH
Anderson? I gave mine up when I married you. And "Atwood" wasn't a small thing to give up. *Pause.* That isn't a winner, is it. Martin could adopt.

EDWIN
No.

SARAH
It would keep the family name going.

EDWIN
It wouldn't be the same.

SARAH
It wouldn't be the same blood line, would it.

EDWIN
No.

SARAH
Oh, actually that's an old-fashioned concept, isn't it. It isn't the blood any more; it wouldn't be your genes, would it. We can make scientific progress in understanding how things work, but somehow it doesn't change our real attitudes, does it. How about Holly. She carries your genes.

EDWIN
So?

SARAH
So she's a girl, but her children will carry your genes.

EDWIN

Not the Y chromosome.

SARAH
Omigod! Is your Y chromosome all we're arguing about here?! Is <u>that</u> why our son is unwelcome in your house?

EDWIN
Don't ask me to accept his ... his lifestyle! Being gay isn't just a choice, it's a decline in moral values! Just talking about this bothers me. I'm gonna go change clothes and go out for a run.

SARAH
Go ahead. I hope it makes you feel better. I hope it clears your mind.

Edwin leaves. Sarah turns to Holly.

Well, we still have most of the afternoon, which is good, because I have to work on our taxes. Were you planning to do anything? *Beat.* Holly! Can you hear me? Would you turn that off, please!

Holly removes the earphones again.

HOLLY
Yes, Mama?

SARAH
I was asking if you have any plans for the rest of the day.

HOLLY
Not really. Do I have to do something?

SARAH
No, I was just asking.

Holly starts to put the earphones back in. Pause.

HOLLY
Mama?

SARAH
Yes, dear?

HOLLY
Do you think Daddy'll ever accept Martin for who he is?

SARAH
I don't know.

HOLLY
You think Martin's okay, right? I mean just like he is? You love him, don't you?

SARAH
Of course.

HOLLY
Why can't Daddy.

SARAH
He still loves Martin. It's just that he thinks being gay is a choice and Martin's making the wrong choice. Some feelings are hard to change.

HOLLY
What if I did something you didn't like. Would I be unwelcome here?

SARAH
You'll always be welcome here.

HOLLY

201

I heard Madison or the state passed a law, sometime, about who you can discriminate against.

SARAH
Whom, whom you can discriminate against.

HOLLY
Whatever. Anyway, it says you can't discriminate against someone for being gay.

SARAH
On the basis of sexual orientation. That's just for employment and certain other things. A law can't change how people think and feel.

HOLLY
I hope I'm never like Daddy with my children. If I ever have any. Who knows, I could turn out to be a lesbian.

SARAH
I don't know if it works that way, but just so you're happy.

HOLLY
Do you suppose people are always like that ... about, you know, about something?

SARAH
Like what.

HOLLY
Prejudiced?

SARAH
Not all people. No, I don't think so. But an awful lot of them.

HOLLY

It changes, doesn't it.

SARAH
What do you mean.

HOLLY
Prejudice. I mean it's, like, different at different times. You know. You know what I mean, don't you?

SARAH
I do. In every generation it's different. Look at your father and me. A lot of people didn't like us being together. Especially not my father, your Grandpa Atwood! Some people still don't, but it's a lot better now.

HOLLY
Mama, besides Grandma and Grandpa Atwood and Grandma and Grandpa Anderson, I don't know much about ... you know, like, about my ancestors. Can you tell me something, or do we have a book somewhere?

SARAH
I'll be glad to sit and tell you what I know, but this is the day I set aside to get our papers in order, so I can do the taxes. We don't have a book, but we do have some boxes of photos and I don't know what else in the attic that came from my grandparents' house. Would you like to look at those?

HOLLY
Oh, yes!

SARAH
Come along. I'll show you.

> *They move from the living room to the attic area. Cross-fade, with lights up on the attic and down on the living room. If the attic complicates the set too*

203

much, a solution like a closet or just a trunk can be worked out.

SARAH
Watch your step. I wonder if this old light still works. You can look through these -- I remember some of them have things written on the back -- but please be very careful.

HOLLY
Oh, I will. Thank you, Mama.

SARAH
Let me know if you find anything interesting. I'll be in the study. See you later.

> *Sarah exits from the attic, through the living room, and out to the study. Holly sits, opens a trunk, and takes out a small album, as the scene below changes from the living room to Camp Randall.*

HOLLY
Oh, Mama, look at this! Look at these people. I wonder who they are.

> *She goes to the light and lies down on the floor to study it. She turns it over and studies the back. Long slow fade in attic. If available, a projection shows the audience the photo Holly sees, of David and Mary Ann and Mary Louise at the Camp Randall hut. Lights up on the same scene.*

Camp Randall; May 16, 1862

Cast: Photographer, John Fuller
        Private Soldier One
        Private Soldier Two
        David Atwood, about 47
        Mary Ann Atwood, about 43
        Mary Louise Atwood, who was 7 but can be played
slightly older
        Mayor Leitch
        Captain Chandler
        J.C. Gregory, 34
        Charlotte Gregory, 42
        Charles Gregory, 11
        Cora, 9
        August Kruer, German
        Michael Zwank, German
        others in street scene

As the lights come up, David, Mary Ann, and Mary Louise Atwood are posing stock-still for a daguerrotype, wearing their Sunday best. People come and go, the more the better, including enlisted soldiers and officers in Union uniform.

PHOTOGRAPHER
Good! That's good. You can relax for a few minutes. I have one more plate.

The Photographer removes a plate from the camera, etc., etc. A Private enters from one side, limping. He crosses in front of the scene. Another private, already onstage, greets him.

ONE
Ned, are you all right?

205

TWO
Yeah.

ONE
You're limping.

TWO
Yeah.

ONE
D'ya get hurt?

TWO
Nah. *[rhymes with "yeah"]*

>   *Long pause.*

ONE
You're limping.

TWO
Yeah.

>   *Long pause. Private One doesn't know what else to*
>   *say, and asks the next question with only his*
>   *outstretched hand and his eyebrows.*

TWO
My number finally came up.

ONE
Wha'd'ya mean. You're still here.

TWO
My number for new shoes.

ONE
Ohhhhh. New shoes. Don't they fit?

TWO
The left one does.

ONE
Why don't you go back and ask for a different right shoe.

TWO
It wouldn't do any good.

ONE
Why not.

TWO
They're all the same.

ONE
They're all the same size?

TWO
Nah, they're different sizes.

ONE
How many'd they send.

TWO
Forty.

ONE
Forty! Maybe I'll get some. If there are twenty pairs, why
didn't you ask for a different one.

TWO
They ain't twenty pairs.

ONE
What?

He looks closely for the first time.

You're wearing two left boots.

TWO
Yeah.

ONE
Why.

TWO
That's all they sent.

ONE
Forty left boots?

TWO
Yeah. I figure I can wear this awhile. If it gets too bad, I'll
go back to my shoe with the hole in it, but maybe this one'll
stretch or I'll get used to it. See, I can walk just fine. *He
starts off.* Hey, you wanna come with me? We got pork 'n'
beans in Company C.

ONE
Pork?! Where'd you get that.

TWO
Well, it ain't actually pork. It's more like 'possum, but the
beans is beans. Come on.

> *They walk off together. The photographer, finished
> with his preparations, motions the Atwoods back
> into position and they comply.*

PHOTOGRAPHER
All right, now. *Pause.* Miss Atwood, would you please …
Missus Atwood, can you ask your daughter to hold still?

MARY ANN
Stop squirming, Mary Louise. You act as if you have ants in
your pants.

DAVID
If you move while he's taking the picture, you'll be blurred in
the photograph.

MARY LOUISE
I know!

PHOTOGRAPHER
That's something I can't guarantee.

DAVID
I know. It's all right. A hundred years from now, when they
look at the records of this time, all babies' faces and all
dogs' tails will be blurred.

MARY LOUISE
I can hold still!

DAVID
Oh right, when you're asleep or dead.

MARY ANN
Don't say that, Mister Atwood.

DAVID
Dead?

MARY ANN
Shhh.

209

DAVID
Oh, don't be superstitious. Talking about something doesn't make it any more likely to happen.

> *Mary Ann breaks the pose, goes to the photographer's camera and "knocks" on it, then returns to her place.*

MARY ANN
Death isn't something to joke about.

DAVID
I don't joke about it, but it isn't a topic to be avoided or ignored. We're surrounded by it, especially here. Almost every day I print a list of soldiers who've died.

MARY ANN
Well, even when it seems commonplace we should treat it with respect and awe. Death is powerful and profound, and we musn't ever let their deaths become routine or unremarkable. *The photographer clears his throat.* I'm sorry. You're ready, aren't you.

> *The photographer answers non-verbally with a facial expression and a nod.*

DAVID
All right.

> *The Atwoods settle into a stiff but pleasant pose.*

PHOTOGRAPHER
That's good. Look at the birdie. Hooold it.

> *He removes the lens cover. Silence for 5 seconds. He replaces the cover.*

There. Done. Thank you.

He begins to pack up.

MARY ANN
Good girl. You hardly moved.

MARY LOUISE
I didn't move at all!

DAVID
Well, I guess we'll know when we get the picture. We'll see
then if your head looks like a cauliflower.

MARY LOUISE
Father!

PHOTOGRAPHER
Your little girl is very becoming. I hope the picture does her
justice. Someday, photography will be less sensitive to
movement.

DAVID
Mister Fuller, do you think it could ever be more sensitive to
movement, and capture it?

PHOTOGRAPHER
Oh, there's always somebody talking about that. One fellow
wants to find out if a horse's hooves are all off the ground
when it gallops, but no-one's been able to prove it either
way. I reckon everybody wants to see their own work
improve. Me, I'd be happy just to get pictures of children
that aren't blurred.

DAVID
Progress is everywhere. I'm a newspaper man. Printing

presses are getting faster and larger.

PHOTOGRAPHER
I predict cameras will get faster and smaller.

DAVID
Wouldn't it be grand if we were able to print photos in a
newspaper.

PHOTOGRAPHER
Not likely.

DAVID
Why not.

PHOTOGRAPHER
It's an entirely different process. If you had to develop and
fix and dry every copy of your newspaper, why, we'd be
reading last week's news.

DAVID
Sometimes we do now. Shut my mouth. Did I say that?
But not the story I came here for today. It'll be in
tomorrow's State Journal.

PHOTOGRAPHER
Poor fellow.

DAVID
Which one, the prisoner or the sentry.

PHOTOGRAPHER
I was thinking of the dead man, but you may be right.

DAVID
Anyway, being able to print photos would really sell
newspapers. I bet some day they'll develop cameras that'll

take photographs right on steel printing plates.

PHOTOGRAPHER
I wouldn't bet on that one.

Mayor William Leitch enters.

MAYOR
Mister Atwood, good afternoon.

DAVID
Mayor Leitch. *[probably pronounced Lite-ch]*

MAYOR
Missus Atwood. Mary Louise.

MARY ANN and MARY LOUISE
Good afternoon, Mayor Leitch.

MAYOR
I expected to see you here today, but not getting your picture taken. Perhaps I'll get a photograph taken, too.

PHOTOGRAPHER
Unfortunately, sir, that was my last plate. Business has been exceptional today. Nothing like a killing to bring out the crowds.

MAYOR
Have you talked to Captain Chandler?

DAVID
First thing this morning, but he didn't want to say anything until after the tribunal.

MAYOR
I've worked with him before. I think we can rely on him to

213

investigate the matter properly and take appropriate action. There he is!

PHOTOGRAPHER
Mister Atwood, is two-ten Monona Avenue your address? I can have it to you by Tuesday.

MAYOR
Oh Captain!

DAVID
That will be fine. Thank you.

MAYOR
He's coming.

PHOTOGRAPHER
Good-bye.

DAVID
Good-bye.

MARY ANN
Good-bye. Thank you.

The photographer leaves.

Mary Louise and I will take a little walk while you converse with the Captain.

DAVID
That's a fine idea.

MARY ANN
It's good to see you, Mayor. Now don't you two get into an argument. *To David.* We'll be back soon. If you aren't here when we return, we can walk home. It's a superb Sunday

for a stroll.

Mary Ann and Mary Louise leave. Captain
Chandler enters.

MAYOR
Captain.
Chandler.

DAVID
Captain

CAPTAIN
Mayor Leitch, Mister Atwood.

DAVID
Has the tribunal ended? Did they …

CAPTAIN
The sentinal did nothing wrong. It was an unfortunate
incident, but he was obeying orders and his conduct was
even exemplary.

David refers to written notes.

DAVID
The sentinal was Private Clarence Wicks? and the prisoner
was Private G. W. Spears, am I right?

CAPTAIN
Yes.

DAVID
And their units?

CAPTAIN
They haven't changed. Wicks is
in the Nineteenth Regiment,
Wisconsin Volunteers,
Company E.

DAVID
Nineteenth
Regiment,

215

All the prisoners are in the First Alabama Infantry Regiment, captured on Island Ten in the Mississippi at Cairo*[pronounced kay-ro]*. Spears was in Company B of that regiment.

Wisconsin Volunteers, Company E. First Alabama Infantry Regiment. Island Ten.

MAYOR
Can you give us any more details?

CAPTAIN
The prisoner Spears and other prisoners advanced on Private Wicks. Spears cursed and threatened Private Wicks, waving a stick or a bone. Very unusual behavior. Not something we've seen here before. The entire incident was witnessed by the next sentry in the line, who was only a score or so yards away. The second sentry urged Private Wicks to follow the standing order to shoot in the face of a threat.

MAYOR
It was a justified shooting, then.

CAPTAIN
Without a doubt.

DAVID
Would you say this is the farthest north a Confederate soldier has been shot and killed in this conflict?

CAPTAIN
I wouldn't know. That may be of interest to the readers of your newspaper, but it doesn't concern me.

DAVID
Are the prisoners getting more restive?

CAPTAIN

216

No. We consider this an isolated incident. There've been no other such threats. Many of the prisoners have even expressed their gratitude for the good treatment they've received, including the visits and generous donations from the people of Madison, but still, Camp Randall was set up as a training camp -- it doesn't have proper facilities for the care of prisoners -- and plans are being made to transfer the rest of our prisoners to Chicago.

DAVID
We're getting telegraph reports that General Stonewall Jackson is headed up the Shenandoah Valley. Do you think he'll invade the North?

CAPTAIN
I have no insight into that theater of the war. Now if you'll excuse me.

DAVID   MAYOR
Thank you, Captain.   Of course. Thank you.

CAPTAIN
It's my pleasure, as well as my duty.

Captain Chandler exits.

DAVID
He appears to be a square fellow.

MAYOR
I agree. Running a prison camp can't be easy. Prisoners dying almost every day of disease and wounds. It's grim duty and he seems to do it well.

DAVID
Then tell me why you're spending the city's money on extra police patrols.

MAYOR
You know as well as I do. The Captain's job is to maintain
order in the camp. Mine is to maintain order in the city.

DAVID
It isn't escapees from the prison you're worried about.

MAYOR
Hardly. No. Despite his best intentions and instructions,
Captain Chandler can't keep everyone in line, and soldiers ...
well, soldiers will be soldiers.

DAVID
You aren't a strong supporter of this war, are you.

MAYOR
You're wrong, Mister Atwood! And I'll sue you if you print
anything to the contrary! I support the war wholeheartedly,
and I have from the beginning, for the preservation of the
Union.

DAVID
But now ...

MAYOR
I am concerned that you and your fellow abolitionists will
succeed in turning it into something we didn't go to war for.
There's even talk that Lincoln will break his promise --

DAVID
-- and free the slaves. Halleluia! What a glorious day in
history that will be!

MAYOR
If he does, it will be a betrayal of those who supported him
and voted for him for the sake of the Union.

218

DAVID
Accomodationist.

MAYOR
Abolitionist.

DAVID
Copperhead!

MAYOR
Radical!

DAVID
Democrat!!

MAYOR
Republican!!

> *Mary Ann and Mary Louise return, followed at a short distance by the Gregorys, J.C., Charlotte, Charles, and Cora.*

MARY ANN
Mister Atwood, you're still here. I met the Gregorys, from church, and they're coming to meet you.

MAYOR
Missus Atwood, I was just leaving. Excuse me.

MARY ANN
Oh, good-bye, Mayor.

DAVID
Good-bye.

> *Mayor Leitch exits.*

219

MARY LOUISE
Mama, can I show the new boy and girl –

MARY ANN
Their names are Charles and Cora.

MARY LOUISE
Can I show Charles and Cora –

MARY ANN
May I show Charles and Cora ....

MARY LOUISE
May I show Charles and Cora the horses we saw in the corral?

MARY ANN
Yes, you may.

Mary Louise runs off.

DAVID
Are you sure it's safe?

MARY ANN
While you were talking with the mayor, we had a very pleasant chat with the regiment's muleskinner, and now he and Mary Louise are fast friends.

DAVID
Really?

MARY ANN
Yes.

DAVID

What do they have in common.

MARY ANN
Horses.

> *Charlotte, Cora, and Mary Louise enter, followed by*
> *J.C. and Charles.*

CORA
Can we?!

CHARLOTTE
Missus Atwood, are you sure it's safe?

MARY ANN
Yes. Just tell them not to go inside the fence.

CHARLOTTE
All right. You may go with Mary Louise to see the horses,
but you heard Missus Atwood. Stay on the outside of the
fence.

CORA
All right!

CHARLOTTE
And Charles, you watch out for your sister.

CHARLES
But they're girls!

CHARLOTTE
Charles!

CHARLES
I will.

221

Cora and Mary Louise run off, taking Charles with them. J.C. and Charlotte go over to the Atwoods.

J.C.
Mister Atwood.

DAVID
Mister Gregory?

They shake hands.

J.C.
My wife, Missus Gregory.

DAVID
Pleased to meet you.

CHARLOTTE
Likewise.

MARY ANN
Mister Atwood said he wanted to meet the new lawyer in town, and here you are.

J.C.
May I offer you a cigar? You don't attend church, sir?

DAVID
Oh, but I do. I'm a member of the Congregational Church, the first church built in town. Our congregation started meeting in the Peck Cabin.

MARY ANN
I so hated to see that go. It <u>was</u> ugly and decrepit and unsafe, but it was the first building in Madison.

DAVID

222

That's progress. People always see progress as positive until they notice that something irreplaceable has been lost.

J.C.
But your wife.

DAVID
My wife? *Beat.* Oh, our churches. Missus Atwood is Episcopalian, as you apparently are. The services aren't so different that I couldn't attend yours, but I'm just more comfortable where I am.

CHARLOTTE
It must have been a challenge to get both your parents' blessings for your marriage.

DAVID
Yes. But after much cajoling and many tears they gave in.

MARY ANN
My parents were sure that Congregationalists were little better than heathens! Mister Atwood likes his own religion, but I think he likes the church itself even better.

DAVID
Missus Atwood! That's secondary. But we did have the finest church in the city.

MARY ANN
Until Grace Episcopal built a more splendid one.

DAVID
At least we still have the largest bell in the city.

    Beat.

J.C.

223

Doesn't he know?

MARY ANN   DAVID
Um ...   Know what!

J.C.
He clears his throat. I hate to be the bearer of bad news, but
Grace Episcopal will soon have a larger bell than you do.

DAVID
Why didn't you tell me.

MARY ANN
I'm sorry. I should have, but I knew it might upset you, and
the time just never seemed right.

DAVID
Upset me?! I'm only upset to be the last to know. A
newspaper man should be the first to know!

J.C.
I'm sorry if I stirred up --

DAVID
Oh, it isn't your fault.

MARY ANN
Don't apologize. He'll get over it very soon, won't you,
Dear.

     Long silence.

CHARLOTTE
Your congregation hosts some of those anti-slavery lectures,
don't they.

DAVID

Indeed we do. We had the honor of hosting Mister Fredrick Douglass some years ago. What a speaker!

CHARLOTTE
And that slave son of President Jefferson was a member of your congregation before he died, wasn't he.

DAVID
Yes. Eston Hemings Jefferson. He's buried in Forest Hill Cemetery here.

CHARLOTTE
Did you ever talk to him about his parentage?

DAVID
No. He was a quiet man, not wanting to draw attention to himself. I never heard anyone ask him directly to discuss his father, but many were the times when someone in conversation would say offhandedly, "your father, President Jefferson", and he would acknowledge it with a nod and a smile.

CHARLOTTE
I suppose it would be easier to acknowledge your heritage as the son of a president than as a slave?

DAVID
He was listed as white in the Virginia census after he was freed.

CHARLOTTE
Still, it would seem ...

DAVID
What is your point, ma'am. We were proud to have him as a member of our congregation, whether he was categorized as black or white or both or neither. And we are proud to have

other representatives of the Negro race in our church.

CHARLOTTE
I'm sorry, I didn't mean to suggest ...

MARY ANN
At least he came of good Colonial stock, didn't he, Mister
Atwood. Not an immigrant, like the Norwegians and the
Germans.

DAVID
That's certain. Tell me, Mister Gregory, did you and Missus
Gregory arrive in Madison on the train?

J.C.
Yes, we did.

DAVID
Well, that railroad's another piece of <u>progress</u> that's been a
mixed blessing. It's brought people like you here, but it's
also brought the immigrants in droves. There were Germans
and Norwegians on the very first train into Madison in '54.
And after that sometimes as many as 300 a day.

MARY ANN
Some moving on, some staying, many arriving already
infected with cholera and who-knows-what, some dying on
the train, some dying at the depot. Children among them.

DAVID
That was when Madison set up the first fire department and
the first board of health.

MARY ANN
Madison was once a beautiful little town.

DAVID

Did you know that Horace Greeley visited here and said it was "the most magnificent site of any inland city I ever saw."

J.C.
We read that. It was one of the reasons we made the decision to come here.

DAVID
Well, he and I may be friends, but if I ever see him again I intend to tell him the worst aphorism he ever uttered was "Go West, young man!" since those who most followed his advice seem to have been Germans and Norwegians.

CHARLOTTE
Do you know Mr. Greeley?

DAVID
Indeed I do. He and I attended school together in New Hampshire.

CHARLOTTE
Really!? You're from New Hampshire!? Did you ever meet Mister Daniel Webster?

DAVID
No, I can't say --

CHARLOTTE
Oh, he's the most wonderful man. I met him when he was campaigning for the United States Senate.

J.C.
My wife was in the best circles of New Hampshire society. She was a personal friend of Dolley Madison.

CHARLOTTE

227

Now don't drop names, Mister Gregory. *Beat.* But I also
knew Missus Alexander Hamilton.

MARY ANN
How wonderful!

CHARLOTTE
And my grandfather fought and died in the Revolutionary
War.

MARY ANN
David's family goes back at least that far, doesn't it, Dear.
His great-great-great-grandfather John Atwood settled in
Plymouth Mass in 1643.

DAVID
Now Missus Atwood, there's no need for us to flaunt our
respective lineages. I figure everyone's family goes back
just as far as any other.

CHARLOTTE
Perhaps, but it makes a difference what nature of people
were in your family tree. People of lineage can afford to say
it doesn't matter. Plymouth! My!

DAVID
Well, at least it wasn't Salem.

J.C.
You said you knew Mister Greeley in New Hampshire. But
I heard you came here from New York.

DAVID
That's right.

J.C.
What were you doing there.

DAVID
That's where I learned the newspaper business. I helped
publish a Whig paper, and I was active in the anti-slavery
movement there.

J.C.
But you're no longer a Whig. I hear you were one of the
founding members of that new Republican Party.

DAVID
Yes, I was. We held our first meeting in Ripon in fifty-four.
Would you care to join?

J.C.
To tell the truth, I haven't been very active in politics.

DAVID
Oh, we can change that. You'll find Madison to be a hotbed
of politics, and a cradle for political ambition. The next time
we get together, I'll tell you more about the Republican
Party. You may yet find it a comfortable home.

Music is heard, as if a marching band is
approaching offstage. The music is a German song.

MARY ANN
Do you hear that?

DAVID
How can I help it!

J.C.
On a Sunday!

CHARLOTTE
What is it.

DAVID
It must be that new band whose advertisement I printed this week: the Madison Musical Society ... all songs in German.

The song ends. August Kruer and Michael Zwank enter.

KRUER
Grüss Gott, Herr Atwood!

DAVID
God would be a lot happier if you'd respect the sabbath!

KRUER
Now just because competitors in the newspaper business are we, you need not complain about our celebrations.

DAVID
Mister Kruer, I have nothing against you for publishing the Staats Zeitung. We don't compete for the same readership. But I do have something against music on Sunday!

KRUER
You have your ways and we have ours.

DAVID
Well, don't ask me to approve of yours. They aren't American, and there's a limit to tolerance when it involves respect for God's sabbath. Good day, Mister Kruer.

KRUER
Guten Tag, Herr Atwood.

The music starts again but fades quickly as the band moves on.

230

ZWANK
Excuse me! Is it true you have sermons in your church
against band music and dancing on Sunday?

DAVID
Yes, we do.

CHARLOTTE
So do we. Just this morning.

ZWANK
Ach! What do you on Sunday afternoons?

DAVID
We study the Bible and contemplate the follies of man.

ZWANK
Ach. I think you and the rest of that Codfish Aristocracy
could use a little more Gemütlichkeit!

DAVID
Who are you, sir?

ZWANK
Zwank ist mein Nam'. Michael Zwank, stone mason. We go
to church on Sundays, but after, we enjoy our families, our
friends, and our music.

CHARLOTTE
And your beer!

ZWANK
Ja, gnädige Frau! Das ist richtig. Gott gave us beer, too.

J.C.
And ten pins?

ZWANK
Yes, we sometimes play those too, but maybe those aren't a
gift from Gott.

DAVID
It looks like the band's leaving you behind. You'd better
catch up. Good day, Mister Zwank.

ZWANK
Viele Dank'! Guten -- Wait! You didn't introduce yourself.

DAVID ATWOOD
David Atwood, editor of the Wisconsin State Journal.

ZWANK
Herrlich! You can report my wedding, next week. I marry a
girl from Germany. You know where that is, Herr Atwood?

DAVID
Yes, I do.

ZWANK
Have you ever been there?

DAVID
No, I haven't.

ZWANK
Schade. Auf wiedersehen, Herr Atwood.

DAVID
Good day, Mr. Zwank.

> Mr. Kruer and Mr. Zwank exit. The music fades in
> the distance.

Well, what do you think of the new addition to the musical

and cultural life of Madison.

CHARLOTTE
Shameful!

J.C.
Disgusting!

MARY ANN
The music?

J.C.
Well, yes, but more importantly, the disrespect! Here we
are, just starting our history as a city, and --

CHARLOTTE
And these godless people who have no respect for our
customs are overrunning the city and the country.

J.C.
Frankly, we worry about the future of Madison, with all
these immigrants.

DAVID
When I came here in '47, the town of Madison had less than
a thousand residents and I knew most of them. Now, with
six thousand, it's too big.

CHARLOTTE
But even more distressing than the growth of the city is the
disintegration of cultural and moral values: dancing and
drinking and playing ten pins on Sunday! Where will it end!
I worry about the future, not just for Madison, but for our
beloved country.

ENTR'ACTE 1

Lights down on the scene and up on the attic. Holly closes the album, sets it aside, and goes downstairs from the attic to the living room.

HOLLY
Mama!

Sarah enters from the kitchen.

SARAH
Yes, dear?

HOLLY
Do you remember the Confederate cemetery we saw? *Sarah nods.* Your great-great-whatever was here in Madison then.

SARAH
Yes?

HOLLY
And that's where they buried the Confederate prisoners who died at Camp Randall.

SARAH
That's right. We learned that on the tour.

HOLLY
Yeah, I guess, but I just saw this picture, and it made it all so much more real. Look.

Holly shows Sarah a photo.

SARAH
I remember looking at that a long time ago. Is that David Atwood?

234

HOLLY
Yes! It says "David and Mary Ann and Mary Louise
Atwood at Camp Randall, May 16, 1862."

SARAH
What a wonderful photo. We really should have it preserved
and framed. It's a shame Mary Louise moved her head. I
wish I could take the time to get into it and see everything
there, as you just did, but I'm so glad you're enjoying this.

HOLLY
There are lots of others, too. Mama, what was that story the
guide told, you know, about some lady taking care of, like,
the graves?

SARAH
Weren't you listening?

HOLLY
Not much, but you should be happy at least I remember he
said something.

SARAH
Well, Alice somebody, Waterman I think he said, was born
in Louisiana and came to Madison just a couple of years
after the Civil War, and she cared for the Confederate
cemetery. She arranged to have the wooden headboards
replaced by stone markers, and had it fenced and beautified,
and she asked to be buried there when she died.

HOLLY
And was she?

SARAH
Yes. People still take care of it. For many years someone
put little Confederate flags on the graves around Memorial

235

Day, a hundred and forty flags. But that stopped a few years ago when somebody complained that the flags created a hostile environment.

HOLLY
That's dumb.

SARAH
Well, I admit I don't care much for the Stars and Bars. I tense up when I see it because it's so divisive and so often used for the wrong things.

HOLLY
Well then, somebody should put something else up every Memorial Day, like a ... you know, a something other than a flag that says "casualty of the civil war".

SARAH
That's a really good idea. Why don't you send it in to the newspaper.

HOLLY
Whatever. You do it. I'm going back upstairs.

SARAH
Okay. Have fun.

HOLLY
I am!

> *Holly returns to the attic and to the trunk. She takes out a fan identical to that used by Mary Louise in scene 2, and a packet of letters. She carries the letters back to the light. She sits on the floor or on something, unties the packet, pulls out one card and reads.*

HOLLY
My dear Mary Louise, I want to thank you for your
friendship, and for confiding your deepest longings with me.
Your thoughts will remain safe with me. Your lifelong
friend, Cora.

> *Holly pick up another envelope, takes out a letter,*
> *and reads.*

HOLLY
Mister and Missus David Atwood, Lewis and Clark Hotel,
Saint Louis, Missouri, November 8, 1883. Dear Mother and
Father, I hope your travels continue pleasurable. I was so
pleased to receive the news that Mother's neurasthenia is
improving. I have mixed news today.

> *Focused light up on Mary Louise, whose voice*
> *blends with and then replaces Holly's.*

You missed the most delightful meeting of the Madison
Literary Club this afternoon ...

MARY LOUISE
You missed the most delightful meeting of the Madison
Literary Club this afternoon, but you also missed one of the
most tragic events in Madison's history.

> *Lights down on the attic and up on the living room,*
> *which is furnished in 1883 style.*

<u>SCENE 2</u>
The Atwood home at 210 Monona Avenue; November 8,
1883

Cast: musician(s)
          Mary Louise Atwood, about 30
          Ella Giles, about 30
          Cora Gregory, about 30
          Charles Gregory, about 30
          Julianna, any age, any race
          William, African-American male
          Michael Zwank, about 50
          Bernard Higgins, about 30
          Photographer
          Frank Lloyd Wright, 16
          others at Literary Club meeting
          others in crowd

*As the lights come up a musician is concluding a
piece. The actual musician(s) can change during the
show's run. If there is no guest performer to thank
by name, Mary Louise should thank "Professor
Parker". The audience includes Mary Louise
Atwood, Cora and Charles Gregory, Ella Giles, and
others. The artist(s) conclude(s) and the audience
applauds.*

MARY LOUISE
Thank you, Professor Parker, the Music program at the
University is indeed lucky to have such an accomplished
performer. We appreciate your agreeing to be the featured
event of our monthly meeting. Please stay. I'm sure the
members of our club would like to talk to you. We saved
you some cake, and it will take us only a few minutes to
conclude our meeting. Miss Giles, would you care to
announce the next one?

238

ELLA GILES
Well, Miss Atwood, I could, but since I'll be the one
speaking ...

MARY LOUISE
Oh, of course. It would be more appropriate for me to make
that announcement. The next meeting of the Madison
Literary Club will be held on Sunday, December fifth, at the
Opera House, and Miss Ella Giles will speak about what
Madison needs most to be a truly capital city. And as long
as I have the floor I will take this opportunity to thank Miss
Giles once again for establishing this club and for her
continuing leadership.

    Applause.

MARY LOUISE
The meeting is adjourned. Thank you all for coming.
Special thanks again to our musician, Professor Parker. I'll
ask Julianna to come and make sure you have everything
you came with.

    Mary Louise rings for Julianna. Everyone gets up,
    mills around, and speaks quietly. Mary Louise and
    Cora and Charles meet near the front of the stage.

CORA
A lovely program.

MARY LOUISE
Cora Dear, I hope you don't have to leave right away. I
haven't seen you, to talk to, in ages. I'd love to have you stay
a little longer.

CORA
Can we? You said you have an appointment, Charles.

CHARLES
It's not for awhile yet. We can stay.

Charles turns to talk to someone and drifts away.

MARY LOUISE
Oh good. Though if we get the chance, I'd like to talk to you privately.

> *Julianna enters. Mary Louise starts to see people out. She can mouth "good-bye" to people as they leave.*

ELLA GILES
Where were Mister and Missus Atwood?

MARY LOUISE
Oh, I must have told the group before you arrived. They haven't returned yet from their Grand Western Tour. They're sorry to be missing this, but when I write them next I'll recount the event for their enjoyment. Did you have the opportunity to hear Ole Bull when he was here?

AUDIENCE MEMBER
Yes, indeed. He was gracious enough to give a short violin recital just for the faculty. Afterward, someone suggested he should bill himself as the Norwegian Paganini, to which he replied with characteristic immodesty, "I would prefer to have people think of Paganini as the Italian Ole Bull."

MARY LOUISE
Well, when you're as accomplished as he is, you can get away with that.

MUSICIAN
Thank you again. Good-bye.

MARY LOUISE
Good-bye.

ELLA GILES
When do they return.

MARY LOUISE
Not for another few weeks.

ELLA GILES
I do hope they'll be here for our next meeting. As you know,
the first item on my list of capital needs is a hospital, and I
want to enlist as much interest and support as I can among
the more influential families for the idea of starting one here.

MARY LOUISE
I'll be sure to remind them of the event in my next letter.
They wouldn't want to miss a lecture by you any more than
they would miss the promised oration by William Jennings
Bryan at next year's Chautauqua.

ELLA GILES
Thank you, but I really shouldn't be linked in the same
sentence with Mister Bryan.

MARY LOUISE
Why not. You're Wisconsin's first published novelist.

ELLA GILES
Thanks in large part to your father's influence. Why, he
practically printed "Bachelor Ben" for me.

MARY LOUISE
Well then, you see the esteem in which he holds you. Oh!

ELLA GILES
What.

MARY LOUISE
It just occurred to me that you should repeat your lecture at
the Chautauqua.

ELLA GILES
That's a good idea. I could expand the topic beyond
Madison but it would fit right in.

MARY LOUISE
That way, even if they do miss next month's meeting ...

ELLA GILES
they could hear it anyway. Clever, Miss Atwood.

MARY LOUISE
The Chautauqua is one event they never miss. They're not
Sunday School teachers --

CORA
Neither are half the people who attend it.

MARY LOUISE
-- but even so, they attend all of the sessions, as they say,
religiously.

Charles drifts back.

ELLA GILES
Your father actually helped start the Chautauqua, didn't he.

MARY LOUISE
Yes, he's quite proud of being one of the Congregational
Church members who voted to invite the Wisconsin Sunday
School Assembly to set up their headquarters here.

CORA

What a change it's made in the city. That and the
Tonyawatha Hotel have turned Madison into a real summer
resort.

MARY LOUISE
With people coming from all over the West.

ELLA GILES
As far away as New Orleans last summer. We had nearly a
thousand visitors last year.

MARY LOUISE
And I'd be willing to bet that many of them found their way
to your lending library.

ELLA GILES
I think a number of them did, and I'm still trying to recover
our only copy of Balzac. Thank you for hosting the event
today.

MARY LOUISE
It was my privilege. This big old house needs people in it.
With just Julianna and me, it feels quite empty. I'm looking
forward to your talk next month.

ELLA GILES
So am I! I have to finish preparing it.

MARY LOUISE
You don't fool me, and you don't worry me. I've never
known you to be unprepared.

ELLA GILES
Thank you for your confidence. It's strange how other
people often have more confidence in a person than he has in
himself. Oh, was that Mister Findorff that just left? Excuse
me. I want to speak to him. Good-bye.

MARY LOUISE
Good-bye.

Ella Giles leaves, pausing at the door to say
something to Julianna. Upon her exit, Julianna
looks at Charles and Cora, sees that they aren't
leaving, and exits. They could sit down.

CHARLES
I overheard the last part of your conversation. Madison
really has become the Athens of the West, at least in the
summer. And now we have the largest assembly hall in the
state ... five thousand people listening to Chautauqua lectures
under one roof without a single pole obstructing anyone's
view. It's a marvel. If he continues putting up buildings like
that, Mister Findorff has a future here.

CORA
There'll be even more summer visitors this year, with the
Columbian Catholic Summer School.

CHARLES
Oh, that's right. They decided to start one, too, didn't they.
Can't they come up with any ideas of their own? Someone
said, imitation is the sincerest form of flattery, but ... really.
It seems like every good idea we have, the Catholics copy it,
but of course they have to be separate.

CORA
Like their cemetery. Such exclusivity. They must think
they're going to a separate heaven.

CHARLES
No, it's not that; they're apparently the <u>only</u> ones going to
heaven.

244

CORA
What I can't understand is why they have separate areas
within the cemetery for the Germans and the Irish. It's as if
they'll go to different places, where they won't have to
associate with each other.

MARY LOUISE
But seriously, don't you think Catholics should have
religious and moral education, too?

CHARLES
Well, I suppose, but that's like asking if the devil should go
to church. Of course, but what good would it do. They'd be
better off learning how to become good citizens than
swearing allegiance to some foreign prince.

MARY LOUISE
The pope isn't really a prince.

CHARLES
Well, according to them he's a prince of the church, and they
shouldn't kowtow to a foreign power. It's un-American.

Mary Louise, agitated, gets up, if seated.

MARY LOUISE
Charles, would you please open a window. It's getting warm
in here.

Charles get up, if seated, moves toward the
audience, and mimes opening a window.

CHARLES
Wise of you to change the subject.

MARY LOUISE
Thank you. How are your parents?

CHARLES
They're both fine. Thank you for asking. Mother and Father
are enjoying the unseasonably warm fall weather.

CORA
Actually, Father's a bit what you'd call crabbed these days.

MARY LOUISE
Over the election?

CHARLES
Yes. He'll sometimes say he should have followed your
father's advice and joined the Republican Party but, as we all
know, his sympathies have always been Democratic, or
worse.

CORA
He said to lose a bid for Congress once was distressing, but
to lose twice was insupportable.

MARY LOUISE
Have you ever thought of politics, Charles?

CHARLES
No! Or if I have thought of it, it's to thank my stars I have
no interest in it. Aristotle said man is a political animal, but
I get enough politics as it is at the Law School.

MARY LOUISE
Don't you enjoy being Dean?

CHARLES
Sometimes.

MARY LOUISE

Did you know Mister La Follette there?

CHARLES
No, he was a student there before I took over. Did you know, my father lent him four hundred dollars to buy the student newspaper?

MARY LOUISE
No. Did he --

CHARLES
Yes, he paid it back.

MARY LOUISE
He's an ambitious man, isn't he.

CHARLES
He certainly is. I don't imagine he'll be content as District Attorney. I think he has his eye on a run for Congress next time.

CORA
At least we can be fairly sure he won't be running against his benefactor.

CHARLES
No, I think Father won't run again. I do know Mr. La Follette's wife well, though. She just graduated.

MARY LOUISE
And I heard she was admitted to practice before the Supreme Court without a fight.

CHARLES
Yes, quite a change from when they turned down Miss Lavinia Goodell. Times have changed. It would appear that women have arrived.

247

MARY LOUISE
What? What did you say?

CHARLES
I said it would appear that women have arrived.

MARY LOUISE
Mister Gregory, I'm afraid women still have a long way to
go.

CHARLES
Hogwash. Women have made tremendous progress, as has
society in general. Surely you're not suggesting women
should be given yet more privileges.

MARY LOUISE
Not more privileges, more rights!

CHARLES
You know, I think this is an example of give some people an
inch and they'll take a mile. Women have achieved more
freedom than they know what to do with.

MARY LOUISE
We are asking for basic human rights.

CHARLES
Oh, come along, what basic human rights don't you have.

MARY LOUISE
Suffrage! The right to vote, among other things!

CHARLES
Why would you want to vote.

MARY LOUISE

248

To protect our interests and to make the world better!

CHARLES
Don't you think you can count on men to do that for you.
We respect you. We revere you. We even put you above
ourselves in many ways.

MARY LOUISE
Mister Gregory!

CHARLES
What do you mean! You are pampered and privileged and
protected.

MARY LOUISE
Mister Gregory! I'm ... I am nearly speechless.

CHARLES
You and Cora don't want to participate in the hurly-burly of
the world.

MARY LOUISE
The hurly-burly of the world, as you call it, would be a lot
more civilized if women participated in it, so yes, we want
to.

CHARLES
But –

MARY LOUISE
Cora and I may be privileged, I grant you that, but what
about all of the women who are not pampered, privileged, or
protected. How can I possibly make you understand!

CORA
It may be hopeless. He really believes what he says.

249

MARY LOUISE
Do you remember the news about a week ago: someone tried
to kill Mister Hiestand, the registrar at the college?

CHARLES
Yes, of course. I know Hiestand well. He was lucky to have
survived. Davenport was the blackguard's name. I believe
he's still locked up for the assault.

MARY LOUISE
Do you remember it was some dispute over Davenport's
wife?

CHARLES
Uh yes, I believe so, yes. Hiestand wasn't having an illicit
liaison with Missus Davenport, was he?

MARY LOUISE
No.

CHARLES
As I remember, Davenport went after Hiestand with a knife,
but why do you mention all this.

MARY LOUISE
Well, I don't suppose there's been much discussion in your
circles about it, but would you like to know what the
"dispute" over the wife was?

CHARLES
If you seem to think it important, yes.

MARY LOUISE
Davenport went after Hiestand with a knife because
Hiestand "interfered" with Davenport as he was whipping his
wife in the front yard.

CHARLES
Hmm. I suppose that just shows you shouldn't get involved in someone else's --

MARY LOUISE
Mister Gregory! Is that your legal analysis of this?!

CHARLES
What do you mean? Hiestand shouldn't have inter --

MARY LOUISE
Shouldn't have tried to stop a man from whipping his wife?!

CHARLES
Of course not. What business was it of Hiestand's?

CORA
Charles, you'd intervene if a man were whipping his <u>dog</u> on the sidewalk!

CHARLES
Oh I don't think so. It's his dog.

MARY LOUISE
And I suppose it's his wife.

> Charles shrugs his shoulders and raises his
> eyebrows but says nothing in response to this
> obvious statement.

CORA
Have you nothing to say?

CHARLES
No, that's the law as well as the natural order of things. Besides, we don't know what she may have done to deserve it.

251

MARY LOUISE
Doesn't it offend you that Davenport was arrested for
assaulting a man, but not for assaulting a woman?

CHARLES
She wasn't a woman, she was his wife. Besides, he went
after Hiestand with a knife, a deadly weapon. He couldn't
kill his wife with a whip, or a switch, or whatever it was.

MARY LOUISE
That's the law, isn't it. As long as the instrument is smaller
than the man's thumb.

CHARLES
Rule of thumb.

MARY LOUISE
You men are hopeless. The time will come, someday, when
women are appreciated as members of the human race, and
not as property.

CHARLES
I'm afraid it's time for me to leave. Shakespeare said
discretion is the better part of valor. I conclude that every
good commander should know when to retreat. You'll be
more comfortable talking about these women's issues
without me.

CORA
I hate to say this, Charles, because you're my brother and I
love you, but you're right. We will.

MARY LOUISE
The time will come when these are not just women's issues.

CHARLES

252

I'll ask William to take me home and then return for you.
Will that be all right?

CORA
Yes, of course.

MARY LOUISE
Oh, did William bring you?

CHARLES
Yes, Father didn't need him today.

MARY LOUISE
My father mentioned some weeks ago he hadn't seen him in
services at the Congregational Church. Are he and Phoebe
all right?

CHARLES
They're fine, but their son's been sick.

MARY LOUISE
Oh no! I know they were so proud of him starting at the
University this year. *She rings for Julianna.* I hope he'll be
all right.

CORA
Father has his own doctor attending him.

MARY LOUISE
Thank goodness! Without a hospital here, that's the only
good alternative.

   Julianna enters.

JULIANNA
Yes, Miss Mary Louise?

MARY LOUISE
Would you ask William to come here, please?

JULIANNA
Yes'm.

Julianna exits.

MARY LOUISE
And how is, oh, I've forgotten the name of their daughter.

CORA
Grace. She's fine. She must be about thirteen now, and she's begun helping her mother serve us at dinner. A very proper child.

Julianna enters, followed by William.

WILLIAM
You wanted to see me, Miss Atwood?

MARY LOUISE
Yes, how is William Junior.

WILLIAM
Thank you for asking, but he's not well. He got chilled and caught catarrh and it settled in his lungs.

MARY LOUISE
Oh, I'm so sorry to hear it. That can be serious. Everyone likes him. Oh, it would be so horrible if ... I wish there were something I could do.

WILLIAM
Mister and Missus Gregory, and Mister Charles and Miss Cora here, are giving him the best treatment possible.

254

MARY LOUISE
I'm glad to hear that, but I wish we had better medical facilities here. You must be distraught.

Pause.

WILLIAM
Miss Mary Louise, Missus Anderson and I already lost three of our children. Every one was like my heart being torn out of my chest. If Will dies .... *Long pause.* Where I grew up – when I grew up, men -- and women -- had to learn how to bow before the injustices of this world. Watching our son get weaker and weaker feels just like that.

MARY LOUISE
I understand. You bear your troubles stocially.

WILLIAM
I am not a stoic. I wouldn't be able to bear them alone. I've learned that pain eventually stops, and the minute it does, life feels good again, but while the pain continues, it hurts beyond bearing sometimes. Jesus helps me carry that burden.

MARY LOUISE
I admire your response to misfortune. There are many who try to dull their pain with anger and strong drink. Julianna, will you give William something to take home with him, for William Junior and for him and Phoebe.

Mary Louise is fighting back tears.

JULIANNA
Yes'm. What shall I give them.

MARY LOUISE
The best food we have. I don't care. You choose it.

255

JULIANNA
Thank you, Miss Mary Louise. I will.

WILLIAM
Thank you, Miss Atwood.

Julianna and William exit.

CHARLES
That was very kind of you. I think I'll sit up front with
William on the way home. On those rare occasions when
we're alone together, I never tire of hearing him talk of life
as a slave, or of joining a Wisconsin unit when it swept
through Tennessee. Don't call Julianna back. I can see
myself out. Thank you for a very entertaining and enjoyable
afternoon, and I apologize for being a legalistic stick-in-the-
mud.

MARY LOUISE
You should, but, other than that, it's always a pleasure to see
you.

CHARLES
I'll send William back for you, Cora. Good-bye.

MARY LOUISE and CORA
Good-bye.

Charles leaves.

MARY LOUISE
Is there any hope.

CORA
For women to be treated equally?

MARY LOUISE
It's been almost forty years now since Seneca Falls, and we still don't have the vote.

CORA
We do what we can. Having a national woman's suffrage convention didn't change anything overnight. We must be oxen yoked to the plough; we must organize, write, speak.

MARY LOUISE
There are days I feel discouraged. We're surrounded by fossilized thinking. When even someone as intelligent as Charles can't see women as people. Why, he's like one of those cavemen they found in the Neanderthal.

CORA
I know. I don't understand. How do you change an attitude like that.

MARY LOUISE
If two women like you and I can't do it, is there any hope?

CORA
I'm afraid he sees us as just two busybodies with too much time on our hands. I think he might be more likely to listen to Miss Giles, not just because she's the first Wisconsinite to publish a novel, but because she has a job. Isn't that ironic? Men seem horrified by the idea of a woman working, but a non-working woman's opinion is just a feather on the wind.

MARY LOUISE
Have you read her latest novel?

CORA
"Maiden Rachel"? Of course.

MARY LOUISE

257

It made me think.

CORA
Think? Of what.

MARY LOUISE
Of me. Of us. You and me. We're both in our thirties now, and yet we're still "maidens", or am I deluding myself to use that word. I suppose the world thinks of us as nothing more than a couple of old spinsters. We both have our father and mother to take care of, but what will become of us some day. We have no one to share our lives with and we'll very likely grow old alone.

CORA
You could marry Charles.

Mary Louise chuckles.

MARY LOUISE
Charles is a good man, a solid man, even with his medieval opinion of women, but the thought doesn't appeal to me. I've liked you and Charles since the first time we met, at Camp Randall. Do you remember that?

CORA
Of course I do. You took me to see the horses.

MARY LOUISE
Oh, I don't really think Charles would beat his wife -- but then, you never know what darkness lives in men's hearts. Still, it's more than just his Neanderthal opinions that keep me from marrying your dear brother. Call me crazy, or foolishly romantic, but I believe I should be in love with the man I marry. I don't believe in marrying for mere convenience. I mean, there should be love. Shouldn't there?

CORA
That's what the best modern novels say, and I agree: there
should be love.

MARY LOUISE
Have you ever been in love?

CORA
I don't think so.

MARY LOUISE
That must mean you haven't.

> *A distant rumbling is heard that builds and dies
> away. Cora goes toward the window (the audience)
> and looks out.*

CORA
What was that! Not thunder.

MARY LOUISE
I don't know. I really can't imagine. It sounded like ice
piling up on the lake.

CORA
Except there's no ice.

MARY LOUISE
Whatever it was, it seems to have stopped. Maybe it was
thunder.

> *They both listen for it again in silence.*

CORA
All this talk of spinsters and love makes me curious. Is there
something on your mind?

259

MARY LOUISE
Can I trust you not to repeat what I tell you?

CORA
Of course.

MARY LOUISE
Cora, I met a man.

CORA
A man? Who? Where? When?

MARY LOUISE
It was just a chance encounter. It's weeks ago now, before
Mother and Father left. I had to deliver something to an
address on Williamson Street and it was a pleasant day, so I
walked, by myself.

CORA
By yourself? On Williamson Street?

MARY LOUISE
Oh now, Cora, Madison is a very safe city -- at least before
dark -- and it's improving by the month. Don't you feel
we've reached a new level of civilization now that the City
Council outlawed keeping cows in the city?

CORA
I most assuredly do.

MARY LOUISE
Well, on this particular occasion, I managed to get myself
rather lost, so I summoned up some courage and decided to
ask someone for assistance.

> *Focused light up on Bernard Higgins, who mimes
> the actions described.*

I tapped a gentleman ever so lightly on the shoulder and when he turned toward me … well, Cora, his eyes met mine in a way I can't remember ever experiencing before, and that moment, for the first time in my life, I was speechless.

CORA
That is very difficult to imagine! To think of you not having anything to say!

MARY LOUISE
Yes, I know…it's almost unbelievable – but, Cora, he made me completely nervous with just one charming smile -- and all at once my insides turned to absolute mush.

COR
Are you saying the two of you fell in love with just one glance?

MARY LOUISE
Oh, that's not likely the case, since we only said a few words to each other, and during most of the time I was extremely flustered, so there's no telling what kind of impression I made...

CORA
I'm sure it's not nearly as bad as you remember it. Was it?

Mary Louise nods.

CORA
Oh, my - Have you seen him again?

Light down on Higgins.

MARY LOUISE
Cora, You DO promise me that you won't repeat this to

261

anyone?

CORA
You have my word.

MARY LOUISE
Well, then, yes – I did see him again…The next day I
thought of an excuse to return to that neighborhood and I
wandered all over. I hardly admit it to myself, let alone
anyone else, but I wanted to see him, talk to him –
coherently, I suppose, and to make a better impression, but
more importantly, I just wanted to see that smile again.

CORA
Well, out with it. DID you ever see him again?

MARY LOUISE
For three whole hours I wandered around Williamson Street.
I almost gave up. I almost gave up lots of times. Maybe I
never would have given up, but then I finally saw him, at the
other end of a block. He seemed to notice me immediately.
He broke away from a group of people and came over to me.
We found a bench and sat and talked for a long time – and
this time, I must say that I managed to come up with rather
intelligent conversation - until I had to return home.

CORA
Well, this is wonderful! I'm thrilled to pieces for you! But
why do you seem so hesitant to talk about this charming and
wonderful man?

MARY LOUISE
Because I knew he was unacceptable.

CORA
Is he ... He isn't colored, is he?

262

MARY LOUISE
No, worse. He's Catholic. *Cora exhibits shock.* He's Irish,
and as soon as I met him, I knew I had to ask if he was
Catholic.

CORA
Maybe he's just from a Catholic family and doesn't really
follow the creed.

MARY LOUISE
I'm afraid not. I asked what church he goes to and he said ...
Saint Raphael's, and he attends regularly.

CORA
Oh no.

MARY LOUISE
He's a Papist.

CORA
Oh, dear Mary Louise!

MARY LOUISE
I know as well as you do how unacceptable it would be to
marry a Catholic, but to show you how distracted I was, I
brought it up that night at supper, after I'd talked to him the
second time.

> *The lighting changes and the voices of David and
> Mary Ann are heard from offstage.*

MARY LOUISE
Mother, Father, I met a very nice man.

MARY ANN
Oh, I'm so pleased. Where did you meet him.

MARY LOUISE
Just on the street, walking. I think you'd like him.

DAVID
In what part of town.

MARY LOUISE
On Williamson Street.

DAVID
Hmm. Is he German?

MARY LOUISE
No.

       Long pause.

He's Irish.

DAVID
Catholic.

MARY LOUISE
Yes.

MARY ANN
Then we don't like him.

MARY LOUISE
Father ...

DAVID
You heard your mother. We don't like him.

MARY LOUISE
Why does he have to be Protestant.

MARY ANN
You can't marry a Catholic!

MARY LOUISE
I don't want to marry him! I just met him.

DAVID
You might.

MARY ANN
You might fall in love with him, and we want to spare you
the pain if you do.

MARY LOUISE
So what if I do. Marrying inside my faith isn't as important
to me as it is to you.

MARY ANN
You don't know what you're saying.

DAVID
Of course it is. It's the most important thing.

MARY LOUISE
What if he'd convert.

MARY ANN
It's not the same.

DAVID
That may be good enough for some, but not for us. Don't
ever ask me to bless a union with a Catholic. It would kill
your mother and me if you even thought about doing it.

The lighting returns to normal.

265

MARY LOUISE
And then he started railing against ten million immigrants to the U.S. in the past thirty years, mostly Catholics, all the Irish and most of the Germans, and how they're responsible for the disintegration of moral values in the country, as well as the catastrophic growth of the city. How he wished Congress had prohibited immigration by Catholics as it just did from criminals, the insane, paupers, and Chinese.

> *A confusion of shouts is heard outside. Julianna enters.*

JULIANNA
Ma'am, some men are asking permission to bring in someone who's been hurt.

MARY LOUISE
All right, let them in.

> *Julianna exits and re-enters a few steps ahead of a crowd of men and boys, among whom are a mortally-injured Michael Zwank, a boy age 16, and a photographer with a camera. Some of them are carrying the badly-mangled and unconscious Bernard Higgins.*

What happened! Not you!

MICHAEL
The Capitol collapsed where we were working on it. This is my friend and workmate. Can you call a doctor?

ONE OF THE MEN
There's no hope for him.

MARY LOUISE
No, I will. Julianna, ring up Doctor Boyd on the telephone.

ONE OF THE MEN
There's no need, Ma'am. All the doctors in the city have been sent for already. There are dozens like this one.

MARY LOUISE
You're hurt, too. Are you all right?

MICHAEL
I … I don't know. I'm afraid …

MARY LOUISE
Oh, you don't look well at all. I wish there were something I could do. Would you be more comfortable in a bed? And … this man …

Bernard moans. Michael goes to his side.

MICHAEL
Bernard, I'm here.

BERNARD
Michael! You're all right?

MICHAEL
[obviously lying] Yes, I am.

BERNARD
Thank God. I'm done for.

> *Bernard reaches for a crucifix hanging around his neck, but he falls unconscious again before he can kiss it. The photographer tries to get an angle for a shot.*

MARY LOUISE
Don't take a photograph here! Have you no human feelings?

267

Go back and take a picture of the Capitol.

PHOTOGRAPHER
I already have, Ma'am.

Projection of the collapsed Capitol wing.

MICHAEL
Where are we.

MARY LOUISE
You're in the home of David Atwood.

MICHAEL
Atwood. I remember that name. Many years ago. Michael
Zwank. He reported my wedding.

MARY LOUISE
Don't exert yourself. Can you carry him into the guest
room? This way.

ONE OF THE MEN
Thank you, Ma'am.

> *Mary Louise leads off and some men, including
> Michael, follow her, carrying Bernard.*

We'd better go back and see if anybody else can be saved.

MARY LOUISE
Oh, if we only had a hospital.

> *They file out. Cora notices the boy, who has sunk
> into a chair.*

CORA
And you, young man. Are you all right? You weren't hurt,

were you?

WRIGHT
No. No, I'm all right. I felt a little sick there for a minute.

CORA
What are you doing here? Shouldn't you be in school?

WRIGHT
I was, Ma'am. I'm at Madison High School, but we all heard the crash and ran out to see. I watched as they pulled him out. There are a dozen or more injured, badly, like him, some already dead. I guess he's going to die? That's what they say.

> *He looks at her. After a moment of righteous denial,*
> *she nods.*

Why do you suppose it happened.

CORA
Why do I suppose it happened? It must have been God's will that they die today.

WRIGHT
No! That's what people say whenever they don't understand something. I don't think it has anything to do with God's will. I mean why do you suppose a building just collapses.

CORA
I thought you were asking why they had to die, and we never know the answers to questions like that. I don't know why a building collapses.

WRIGHT
But we can know the answers to things like that. Wasn't it designed properly? Wasn't it built right? Someone must

269

have made a human mistake. That shouldn't have happened. Excuse me, Ma'am, I'm feeling better now. I'll go back and see if I can help. Is this your house?

CORA
No. It belongs to the Atwoods. My name is Cora Gregory.

WRIGHT
Pleased to meet you. Mine's Wright, Frank Lloyd Wright.

CORA
I hope you find the answers to some of those questions.

WRIGHT
I will. Good day.

> *Wright exits and Cora exits toward the guest bedroom. Lights down on the living room and up on the attic.*

ENTR'ACTE 2

HOLLY
I know you will be deeply saddened when you return from
your trip to see the devastation at the Capitol. I am sorry to
end this letter on that note, but any attempt to lighten the air
of disaster felt here today would be false. I can only say that
I miss you terribly and look forward to seeing you again
soon. With love, your daughter Mary Louise. Wow!

> *Holly puts the letter into its envelope and carefully
> ties up the parcel again. She stands, picks up the
> album, and goes to the stairs. Lights up very dimly
> on the living room.*

HOLLY
Mama!

> *Sarah enters. The living room remains dimly lit
> except for the area around Sarah and Holly.*

HOLLY
Mama, I have to show you what I found!

> *Sarah and Holly exit. Lights down.*

INTERMISSION

The Greenbush, October 11, 1922

Cast: Anna, an Italian girl
           Nina and Teodoro Paratore, an Italian couple
           Ethel Anderson, an African-American woman
           Rachel Jastrow, a Jewish woman
           Nick, an Italian boy
           other Italians, Jews and African-Americans,
                  especially two women street entertainers
           David Charles Atwood, about 37
           Judge Ole Stolen, about 40
           John ("Snowball") Riley, African-American
           Photographer

The scene is a small park area bordered by poor but not run-down buildings. Before the lights come up, two street entertainers in festive Italian dress work the audience, and then begin singing Italian street music, preferably with an accordion. (Dancing optional.) Sometime here the photographer enters, asks non-verbal permission to take a photo, gets the permission, takes one or two shots, then leaves. After awhile the Italian street music is joined by a Jewish synagogue chant. These two are then joined by African-American gospel music from a church choir rehearsal. [Ideal: they start as overlapping cacophony and end as interweaving harmony.] The music ends. Lights up.

Nina and Teodoro bring on decorations/preparations for Columbus Day.

NINA
You look good for tomorrow.

GIRL ONE

Grazie, Signora Paratore.

GIRL TWO
Will you dance with us tomorrow?

NINA
I will, and I think my husband will, too, won't you, Teodoro.

TEODORO
We will see. We will see how good your music is.

GIRL TWO
The music will lift you out of your seat.

GIRL ONE
Your feet will start moving by themselves.

The girls circle Teodoro.

GIRL ONE
You will be transported back to Italy.

TEODORO
To Sicily.

GIRL TWO
Palermo?

TEODORO
Si!

GIRL ONE
You will feel as if you never left. You will be a young man
again, dancing in all the joy of youth, when dancing is the
purpose of life.

TEODORO

Then you will see me dance.

Girl One and Girl Two exit.

NINA
Do you have the Bersagliere banner there?

TEODORO
No, I bring that tomorrow.

NINA
Do you think it's safe to leave our house with so many people in it?

TEODORO
Tony and Vito are there. There is never any trouble.

Anna comes skipping out of a storefront, followed by Ethel and other African-Americans if available. Anna runs over to Nina and Teodoro. Ethel follows her over.

ANNA
Mama, Papa!

NINA
Ciao, Anna.

TEODORO
Ciao, ragazza.

ANNA
Can I help?

NINA
Si, certo. Missus Stassi has the tablecloths. You can go to her house and help her get them and bring them to the park.

TEODORO
Do you think it will be safe to leave the tablecloths there tonight?

NINA
It won't rain. We can leave them folded up on the tables. No-one will take them.

ETHEL
Hello. You're Mister and Missus Paratore, aren't you.

NINA
Yes. Hello. You're Miss Anderson. You're the minister of the church!

ETHEL
Yes. Is this your daughter?

NINA
Si, signora. Where have you seen this child.

ETHEL
Oh, she sometimes comes to our church.

NINA   TEODORO
Your church!   Your church?

ETHEL
Yes. She likes to sing in our choir with us.

NINA
Does she behave herself?

ETHEL
Oh yes, she's a wonderful child. And she sings loud.

275

ANNA
Can I show them?

Anna and Ethel sing a snatch of gospel.

NINA
Che bello! She is welcome to sing with you.

TEODORO
Aren't you worried she won't grow up a good Catholic?

NINA
She is learning other things there, and she's still learning all
the Jesus songs. It will be all right. *To Anna.* Go on. Go to
Missus Stassi's, and if you see your lazy sisters, tell them to
help you.

ANNA
Yes, Mama.

Anna exits.

ETHEL
You're preparing for Columbus Day?

NINA
Si.

ETHEL
That's a big day for Italians, isn't it.

TEODORO
Si. Where would all of you be if we Italians hadn't
discovered America. *Beat.* Excuse me, that's maybe a hard
question for you.

ETHEL

Some say America was invaded, not discovered.

TEODORO
Anyway, tomorrow we rename Brittingham Park Columbus
Park.

ETHEL
We'll come and celebrate it with you.

NINA
Grazie.

> *An Italian boy runs across the stage carrying*
> *sausages.*

TEODORO
Alto! *The boy hesitates, but doesn't stop.* Alto! *He stops.*
You're Pietro Bongiovanni's boy, aren't you.

BOY
Si, signore.

TEODORO
Why are you running. What have you taken. Ven ca.

BOY
Only some sausages from Mister Amato. He doesn't mind.

TEODORO
If he doesn't mind, then why are you running. Come. We
will take them back to him and see if he minds. And I will
also tell your papa and your mama and see what they have to
say.

BOY
Ahhh.

277

TEODORO
Come.

Teodoro gestures and leads and the boy follows.

NINA
That Nick is a good boy. He will learn. All children have to learn. I have two sons and four daughters, and they are still learning to be good Italians and good Americans. Are you married?

ETHEL
No, but I have a brother and a sister, and they have children. I enjoy being an aunt.

NINA
Are you family to William and Phoebe Anderson?

ETHEL
They were my grandparents, though they were more like my parents. They took care of me and my brother and sister after my mother died. Her name was Grace.

Rachel Jastrow enters.

RACHEL
Missus Paratore.

NINA
Missus Jastrow.

RACHEL
I made some knishes for your celebration tomorrow.

NINA
Mille grazie. Missus Jastrow, Missus Anderson.

278

RACHEL
Pleased to meet you.

ETHEL
Likewise.

NINA
It's good to see you, but what brings you to our humble
neighborhood.

RACHEL
I just thought I'd stop by and spend some time with my
friends here in the Bush.

NINA
You know you're always welcome here.

RACHEL
I know. That's why I'm here. I know I'm welcome.

ETHEL
Is something wrong?

RACHEL
Do you know the Madison Woman's Club?

NINA
The fine uptown ladies like you, they built the hospital, yes?

RACHEL
They started it.

ETHEL
You're a member, aren't you.

RACHEL
I was. I was one of the charter members and president for a

term, but I was just asked to leave.

ETHEL
But ... why.

RACHEL
They won't say it, but I was the only Jewish member, and I
was the only one asked to leave.

ETHEL
Because you're a Jew? Even after your international
success?

RACHEL
That must have been less important in their eyes than
something else.

Teodoro re-enters.

ETHEL
Were you at their meeting – when was it – back in January?
– when the Ku Klux Klan made a presentation?

RACHEL
No, I boycotted it. Maybe I should have been there. I don't
like the effect they're having here. It is so difficult to be the
object of hatred and discrimination. One doesn't want to be
the one to point it out, and one keeps hoping one's friends
will speak up.

ETHEL
The newspapers here criticize the Klan, but it seems the
more they're attacked in the press, the stronger they become
and the faster they grow.

RACHEL
When I pass my so-called friends on the street now, it's so

difficult. I thought we were friends and I of course accepted them, when I thought they accepted me, but now I find it hard to tolerate the intolerant. So I do feel more welcome here.

NINA
In the Bush, we're all in the same boat, and the name of the boat is poverty. The rest of Madison, uptown, doesn't have to face that.

TEODORO
Oh, some of the Germans got to face it during the war. You know, they had to register as aliens and turn in their guns.

ETHEL
Schools stopped teaching German.

TEODORO
I even know one German who was called in to court and questioned as a traitor 'cause he said there might be two sides to the war.

NINA
Well, thank God the war's over now, almost four years now. May it really have been the war to end wars.

David Charles Atwood enters.

TEODORO
Buona sera, signore Atwood.

DAVID CHARLES
Good evening, Mister Paratore.

TEODORO
There is a crowd at the bar already.

DAVID CHARLES
Thank you. Will I see you there?

TEODORO
Not tonight. My wife and I, we are preparing for Columbus
Day celebration tomorrow.

DAVID CHARLES
Oh, will it be here?

TEODORO
In Columbus Park.

DAVID CHARLES
Where?

TEODORO
Brittingham Park.

DAVID CHARLES
Oh, I see. Would it be all right if I come and bring my wife?

TEODORO
Ma certo! All are welcome.

DAVID CHARLES
Thank you.

TEODORO
Did you know that America is named after an Italian?

DAVID CHARLES
Yes, Amerigo Vespucci.

TEODORO *correcting the pronunciation*
Vespucci. Where would all of you be if we Italians hadn't
discovered America.

DAVID CHARLES
Back in England, I guess.

TEODORO
I'm going to the house to get the chairs for the band.

DAVID CHARLES
I'll go with you.

     Teodoro and David Charles start to exit.

ETHEL
Excuse me. Mister Atwood?

DAVID CHARLES
Yes?

ETHEL
I'm Ethel Anderson.

     David Charles waves Teodoro on and he exits.

DAVID CHARLES
Pleased to meet you. As you seem to know, I'm David Charles Atwood.

ETHEL
Are you kin to Mary Louise Atwood?

DAVID CHARLES
Yes, she's my aunt. Why.

ETHEL
This is Missus Rachel Jastrow.

DAVID CHARLES

283

I'm pleased to meet you. I've read a lot about you. You represented the United States in Belgrade, didn't you.

RACHEL
Budapest.

DAVID CHARLES
Budapest. I read about your trip and your speech.

RACHEL
Pleased to meet you.

DAVID CHARLES
I also have copies of your books. You translated one from German and one from French. That's very impressive.

RACHEL
Thank you.

ETHEL
It appears your aunt dropped Missus Jastrow from the Madison Woman's Club.

DAVID CHARLES
Really?

RACHEL
Well, I was asked to submit my resignation.

DAVID CHARLES
Was any reason given?

RACHEL
No.

DAVID CHARLES
I don't think she would have asked you to leave without

some good reason.

RACHEL
None was given, and I know of none.

ETHEL
Missus Jastrow is Jewish, the only Jewish member of the club, and times being what they are ....

DAVID CHARLES
Oh, I see. I understand your concern, but I don't think my aunt would have asked you to leave just because you're Jewish. She's never ... I don't think ... My venerable aunt has always held very progressive views, but ... *Long pause.* the club as a whole must have pressured her to do it.

Ole Stolen enters.

OLE
Mister Atwood!

DAVID CHARLES
Mister Stolen. Or should I say, Judge Stolen.

OLE
You can wait until after I'm elected.

DAVID CHARLES
With all the publicity you got for freeing Dogskin Johnson, is there any doubt?

OLE
I worry, especially this year with women voting. What brings you here.

DAVID CHARLES
The same thing as you, probably. The best liquor in

285

Madison.

OLE
Valenti's.

DAVID CHARLES
Paratore's. May I introduce you to Missus Jastrow, Missus
An --

OLE
No need. Where is Paratore's?

DAVID CHARLES
Excuse me, ladies. It's in the next block. Eight eighteen
Regent Street.

The women move aside to talk among themselves.

OLE
I telephoned your house, asked for you and, can you believe
it, your wife told me I might find you here.

DAVID CHARLES
What do you mean "can I believe it".

OLE
Well, she seemed to treat it as .... You actually told her you
were coming to the Greenbush?

DAVID CHARLES
Of course. You wouldn't?

OLE
Not on your life.

DAVID CHARLES
Where are you, then.

286

OLE
I'm working late.

DAVID CHARLES
You must work late often.

OLE
I do. There's no end to the work. The law is a strict
taskmistress.

DAVID CHARLES
What would happen if she tried to telephone you at your
office.

OLE
I've told her not to do that, that when I work late I need to
concentrate. But I make it a point of calling her once in
awhile.

DAVID CHARLES
Is there a telephone in Greenbush?

OLE
There's one at Schwartz's Drugstore.

DAVID CHARLES
That's good to know.

OLE
Or, if it's too loud there, you can walk a couple more blocks
to Madison General.

DAVID CHARLES
Of course.

OLE
Why they put the hospital in this God-forsaken
neighborhood I'll never understand.

DAVID CHARLES
It was the only place the neighbors didn't object.

OLE
I still don't see why we taxpayers should have to support a
hospital for the general public.

DAVID CHARLES
Most of the cost was raised by the Woman's Club and other
private donors. Would you prefer our tax money to be spent
on something like a community auditorium?

OLE
Something like that monstrosity designed by what's-his-
name! Not on your life!

DAVID CHARLES
Wright.

OLE
Who?

DAVID CHARLES
Frank Lloyd Wright.

OLE
I'd rather pour my money down the sink than support that.

DAVID CHARLES
Speaking of pouring, I was going to take you to Paratore's.

OLE
Yes. Lead on. I must say, of all the laws we have to deal

288

with, prohibition is the stupidest.

They start walking, but Ole stops every few steps.

DAVID CHARLES
It certainly seems to be the least enforceable.

OLE
Trying to get a man to pass up strong drink is like forcing a
pig to pass up mud.   When I'm elected judge, I intend to ....
Speaking of mud, *He stops and looks around.* do you
suppose this is how they all live back in Italy or wherever
they come from?

DAVID CHARLES
I don't think so. I understand the Greenbush used to be a
marsh that was filled in -- just barely -- with ashes and other
trash.

OLE
How can they stand to live like this?

DAVID CHARLES
I don't think most of them have much choice. This is the
cheapest area in the city to live. Houses that aren't wanted
elsewhere are picked up and brought here. Some of them
aren't even hooked up to water and sewer lines.

OLE
That makes it a breeding ground for disease and poverty and
crime. *He stops.* This is where Annie Lemberger lived, isn't
it.

DAVID CHARLES
Yes, I believe so, at Frances and Regent Streets.

OLE

And her naked body was found floating in Monona Bay right over there.

DAVID CHARLES
I don't remember that it was naked.

OLE
I do hope uncovering her true murderer will serve me well in the election. By the way, would you care to contribute to my campaign?

DAVID CHARLES
Uh, having an office of public trust, I feel I should avoid taking sides in elections.

OLE
Being head of the State Printing Board is hardly an office of public trust.

DAVID CHARLES
I beg your pardon.

OLE
It's not elected.

DAVID CHARLES
But I am nevertheless expected to follow high ethical standards in my office and avoid undue influences.

OLE
That needn't prevent you from making a small contribution to my campaign … small or large.

DAVID CHARLES
I have to decline, as a matter of principle.

John enters, well-dressed, sees the two groups, and joins the women.

OLE
Well then, what about your wife. Could she make a contribution?

Beat.

DAVID CHARLES
I'll ask her.

OLE
And ask how she intends to vote and what's important to her as a woman. Is it the candidate's looks, or his stand on public morality, or what.

DAVID CHARLES
I'm afraid I can't tell you whom she'll vote for, other than Senator La Follette – we both like Fighting Bob -- but she takes her right to a secret ballot very seriously, so I doubt she'll tell me. Her sewing circle stopped talking about recipes weeks ago and they've been talking about nothing but the various candidates and their platforms. I think they'll be the best-informed voters at the polls.

OLE
That's worrisome. I have no idea how to appeal to the feminine mind.

DAVID CHARLES
The participation of women in the electoral process does make a difference, doesn't it, just as they always said it would.

OLE
Do you think I should take a position <u>for</u> or <u>against</u> strict

291

enforcement of prohibition.

DAVID CHARLES
I think you should express your opinion, whatever it is.

OLE
Don't be a blockhead. *raising his voice* In my opinion,
woman suffrage is the worst law ever passed in this country,
and I'm especially embarrassed that Wisconsin was the first
state in the Union to ratify it. Asking women to vote is like
asking pigs to fly. It's bad enough that we allow ignorant
peasants like the wops and kikes that live here in the Bush to
—

JOHN
Mister! You can take that language and that attitude
somewhere else. We don't use those names here.

OLE
Who the hell are you!

JOHN
It's of no matter to you, but my name is John Riley.

OLE
Well, Mister John Riley, I am Attorney Ole Stolen and if I'm
elected judge, you better never appear in my courtroom —

JOHN
Judge? Well now, that doesn't change a thing. People may
act like you in other parts of Madison, but not here in
Greenbush. I think you should leave.

OLE
You and what army are going to make me.

JOHN

You'll be amazed at the army that shows up to help me if you start something, but I can do it myself if I have to.

OLE
You nigger scum!

Ole Stolen steps toward him and David Charles restrains him. John steps forward and all three women restrain him.

DAVID CHARLES
Ole, stop! Mister Riley, let me take care of this. Let's leave.

David Charles drags Ole Stolen off.

NINA
Well done! We don't get that much respect, but you showed him! Mister Riley --

JOHN
You can call me John.

NINA
Well, Mister John Riley, I want you to sit at our table tomorrow!

JOHN
Grazie!

Exit.

ENTR'ACTE 3

Lights down on the scene. Sarah and Holly enter together from the kitchen. As before, the stage remains dimly lit except for the area around Sarah and Holly.

HOLLY
I never heard anything before about the -- what do you call it, the Bush, the Greenbush?

SARAH
We used both names.

HOLLY
You didn't live there.

SARAH
Heavens, no! But some of your father's family did. And my grandfather used to go there during Prohibition, on occasion, to visit the speakeasies.

HOLLY
Speakeasy. Was that like a bar?

SARAH
An illegal bar, so it had to be kept quiet. Lots of people during Prohibition made their own wine or beer or bathtub gin, but some of the Italians and others in Greenbush had connections with suppliers in Chicago, so they had quality alcohol.

HOLLY
But it was illegal?

SARAH
Yes.

HOLLY
Didn't they, like, you know .... Didn't they have trouble with
the police?

SARAH
Well, yes. Police tried to enforce the laws, but it was almost
hopeless. The idea behind Prohibition was noble, I suppose,
to save people from themselves, but human nature being
what it is, a war on alcohol can't be won.

HOLLY
Like the war on drugs?

SARAH
A lot like the war on drugs. Some things were harmless, like
the neighborhood speakeasies in the Bush, but some of it
was deadly, like rival gangs fighting for territory. If I
remember correctly, three policemen and twelve Italians
were shot to death in the Bush during Prohibition.

HOLLY
It's gone now, right?

SARAH
Prohibition was repealed in -- Oh, the Bush. Yes, it was
replaced by public housing projects.

HOLLY
Isn't that good?

SARAH
It depends on your point of view. The housing in the Bush
was substandard by any measure. It was often referred to as
Madison's slum, but there's still a lot of nostalgia for a
community way of life there that disappeared forever. It had
its rough edges, which may have been what kept people from

understanding the core, but memory and nostalgia tend to take away the rough edges. There are only a few reminders of the Greenbush community left.

HOLLY
Like what.

SARAH
The Italian Workmen's Club.

HOLLY
Oh, I've seen that funny old building.

SARAH
It's one of the oldest clubs of its kind in the U.S.

HOLLY
Anything else?

SARAH
There's still one house on the north side of Regent Street that wasn't demolished. It belonged to the Paratore family.

HOLLY
But isn't better housing, like, better.

SARAH
Yes, but it was built with no consideration for the people living there. Instead of helping the displaced people create a new community, or even find adequate housing, the city simply paid the owners, who may not have been the ones living there, condemned the properties, and left everyone to fend for themselves.

HOLLY
And now they're ....

SARAH
All scattered.

HOLLY
Do you remember the graves we saw of an African-
American father and son?

SARAH
Yes. What was their name?

HOLLY
The Hendersons. At first I thought he said "Anderson", so I
was listening. The guide said they were killed by a white
man, didn't he?

SARAH
Yes.

HOLLY
In Greenbush?

SARAH
No, not there. The Hendersons actually had a farm just
south of town. They were shot by their white neighbor there.

HOLLY
Oh no.

SARAH
Your father told me about that when we first met.

HOLLY
I want to go back to those treasures in the trunk, in my
treasure chest!

SARAH
All right. I'll go with you.

Lights up in attic as Sarah and Holly ascend. Lights down in the living room.
They look in the trunk again.

HOLLY
But that's almost all there is.

SARAH
Would you like to see some pictures of your father and me?

HOLLY
Oh yes!

SARAH
I should be able to find them.

> *Sarah looks around, finds a cardboard box, opens it, and takes out some things.*

Here. You can look at these photos. Oh, and look at these!

HOLLY
Old records? What did they call them?

SARAH
Forty-fives! Oh, there are some great songs here: [Blue Moon, or I Want to Hold Your Hand, or whatever the director chooses].

> *[Possible music and dance: Sarah unearths a 45-rpm record player, plugs it in, puts a record on, and they dance.]*

And look at this!

> *She takes out a small snapshot.*

298

HOLLY
What's that.

SARAH
Richard the Third! Does that bring back memories! I'll have
to show this to your father when he gets back.

HOLLY
Is that you?

SARAH
Yes.

HOLLY
You look … young.

SARAH
We were once, believe it or not.

HOLLY
You were in the same play together?

SARAH
Yes.

HOLLY
Is that how you and Daddy met?

SARAH
No. Didn't I ever tell you how we met.

HOLLY
I don't remember.

SARAH
It's a good story, at least I think so. We were both working

299

for the Fair Housing Ordinance, and we met the night the City Council voted on it.

HOLLY
That sounds boring.

SARAH
How can you ...! Well, I guess some of the most important things don't sound exciting unless you're involved in them. Maybe someday you'll get caught up in something and really care about it, something like a presidential election.

HOLLY
Whatever. So all right, what was the Fair Housing whatever-it-was.

SARAH
The Madison Fair Housing Ordinance. It was about being fair to people, mostly people of color, who wanted to buy houses.

HOLLY
So what wasn't fair.

SARAH
People wouldn't sell to blacks.

HOLLY
Like Daddy?

SARAH
Well, he was too young to buy a house then. But we were working for the principle of the thing.

HOLLY
And the play?

SARAH
The play? Oh, that was a few years later, after we were
married, with the Madison Theatre Guild.

HOLLY
You were actors?!

SARAH
Can you believe it?

HOLLY
No way!

SARAH
Holly!

HOLLY
Sorry. My bad.

SARAH
We were pretty good, if I do say so myself.

> *The lighting changes as in scene 2 to indicate a*
> *flashback. Edwin appears in Shakespearean*
> *costume.*

SARAH
I would I knew thy heart.

EDWIN
'Tis figured in my tongue.

SARAH
I fear me both are false.

EDWIN
Then never was man true. But shall I live in hope?

SARAH
All men, I hope, live so.

EDWIN
Vouchsafe to wear this ring.

SARAH
To take is not to give.

EDWIN
Look how my ring encompasseth thy finger.
Even so thy breast encloseth my poor heart.
Wear both of them, for both of them are thine.

The lighting returns to normal.]

SARAH
Maybe we'll do it again, just to show you. I bet they need
older actors and actresses sometimes.

HOLLY
Don't!

SARAH
Why not. Wouldn't you enjoy seeing us on stage, maybe
something like "Our Town". We could be Mister and
Missus what's-their-names.

HOLLY
Not! Hopefully, you'll avoid embarrassing me to death.

SARAH
Not if we're good. *Long pause in which Holly doesn't
answer.* Look, here are some more snapshots you can look
at. There are some letters here, too, but I'm not sure I'm
ready to have you read those yet.

Lights up dim on the living room. Sarah leaves down the stairs carrying the letters, through the living room and out the kitchen exit.

HOLLY
Mama and Daddy? Are they like historical people, too? *Pause.* Will somebody look in a trunk in an attic in fifty or a hundred and fifty years and think my life was interesting and exciting?

She picks up the photos. Cross-fade. Lights down in the attic and up on Scene 4.

SCENE 4
The hallway outside the Madison City Council chamber;
December 10, 1963

Cast: Sarah, the same Caucasian female as in the
                Prologue, but here about 17
           Kate, a high school girl
           George, a Caucasian high school boy
           Edwin, the same African-American male as in the
                Prologue, but here about 17
           Howard Atwood, Sarah's father, about 40
           Photographer
           Fran Remeika
           Others

*Important-looking people and common people enter
and exit, come and go through the chamber doors,
center. Sarah and Kate, high school girls, enter
from the side. A man enters, followed by a mother
and her daughter.*

DAUGHTER
Mom, we are so lost!

MOTHER
Excuse me, sir. Do you know where the Madison City
Council chambers are?

MAN
Yes. Follow me.

They exit across the stage.

KATE
Aren't you worried your father'll see you here?

SARAH

304

Nah, I'm sure he's already in there, wheeling and dealing the City Council members.

KATE
How do you think the vote'll go.

SARAH
You know as well as I do. The people we talk to -- the people who'll talk to us – are all in favor of it. It's all the people who don't talk to us I'm worried about.

KATE
It's just gotta pass! It would be the first one in ... is it the country, or the state?

SARAH
The state.

KATE
It's gotta pass here. Madison's the most liberal city in the state.

SARAH
You know what the rest of the state calls Madison, don't you?

KATE
Thirty square miles surrounded by reality.

SARAH
My father actually thinks it's the opposite, that there's this solid conservative core in Madison surrounded by an ultra-liberal loony fringe, sort of like solar flares around the sun.

KATE
Even if your father doesn't see you here, aren't you afraid he'll find out what you're doing?

SARAH
I care. He already knows what I think.

KATE
He does?

SARAH
We argue all the time. He's so wrong, he makes me want to explode sometimes.

> *Howard enters. [Howard is the generational equivalent of David Carpenter Atwood, who was coroner of Madison, not a real estate broker, and who died in 1960. Sarah is the generational equivalent of Priscilla Ann Atwood, who was a high school student and an apprentice member of the Madison Theatre Guild in 1948.]*

HOWARD
Sarah, what are you doing here.

SARAH
I ... I wanted to hear how the Council vote goes.

HOWARD
You aren't going to speak in favor of the Ordinance, are you?

SARAH
No, I couldn't do that to you.

HOWARD
But you support it, don't you.

SARAH
Have we been over this before? Does my Maidenform support me, or do your Arrow socks support you?

HOWARD
Don't be flippant with me!

SARAH
I'm trying not to get into an argument with you. This is my
friend, Kate.

HOWARD
Hello, Kate.

KATE
Hello, Mister Atwood.

SARAH
Do you really have to be the one to present the Board of
Realtors' position? Why can't you let somebody else be the
spokesperson for intolerance?

HOWARD
Sarah! I am not being intolerant. I'm as willing as anybody
in this city to recognize their rights, but I'm just being
realistic. You know what can happen to a neighborhood if
Negroes move into it. Property values plummet, and all the
decent folk in the neighborhood see their investments melt
away. Why, if we sold a house in Hill Farms to a Negro,
mark my words, within ten years, it'd become another
Greenbush.

SARAH
That's crazy! You predicted the same thing when Carson
Gulley moved into Crestwood.

HOWARD
Crestwood must be filled with fuzzy-headed liberals. That
wouldn't be true in other neighborhoods. The Whites
wouldn't stay in Hill Farms, or Shorewood Hills or Maple

Bluff if Negroes moved in.

SARAH
That's absurd. Do you really think all Negroes are shiftless
and irresponsible, and all whites are good solid citizens and
responsible model homeowners?

HOWARD
No, I don't, but other people do, and that's what this is about.
The issue's economic, not social.

SARAH
You think keeping Negroes out of some neighborhoods isn't
a social issue.

HOWARD
The city has no right to pass an ordinance forcing us to sell
homes to Negroes.

SARAH
It doesn't force anybody to sell homes to Negroes.

HAROLD
It takes away freedom of choice.

SARAH
For the sellers! You want freedom of choice to sell, but not
freedom of choice to buy.
And why did you ever place that stupid ad, the Property
Owners' Bill of Rights.

HOWARD
I placed it on behalf of the entire Realtors Association, and
I'm proud of it. It speaks of our American freedoms.

SARAH
Oh come off it, to protect one of our most precious

308

freedoms, the right to own private property? That is just prejudice painted as patriotism.

HOWARD
Are you a communist now?

SARAH
No, it's just the way you twist things. "The sacred right of private property is meaningless without the right to <u>dispose</u> of it any way the owner chooses, to sell it or to rent it to whoever the owner chooses." By the way, it should be "whomever".

HOWARD
What good is the right to own property if the government tells me who I have to sell it to.

SARAH
The government isn't gonna tell you who -- whom -- you have to sell it to. You just have to sell to the person who makes the best offer, without regard for the color of his skin!

HOWARD
Madison is a city of a hundred and fifty thousand now. There are plenty of places for them to live.

SARAH
As long as they stay out of the better neighborhoods.

HOWARD
Sarah, you don't understand these things!

SARAH
Don't try to dismiss me just because I'm young and I'm your daughter! I may just understand this better than you do!

Howard considers smacking her but is deterred by

309

the presence of others.

I understand there's a prominent realtor or two who don't agree with you.

HOWARD
You're referring to Pat Lucey?

SARAH
Yes! I heard he's planning to appear at the meeting tonight and say the ad doesn't speak for him, and he objects to his realtor's dues going to pay for it.

HOWARD
Well, I don't expect his lone voice'll carry much weight. It's not like he's the governor.

Fran Remeika enters.

FRAN
Mister Atwood.

HOWARD
Missus Remeika.

FRAN
I assume you're here against the Ordinance.

HOWARD
Yes. Are you supporting it?

FRAN
Of course.

HOWARD
Didn't you learn anything from having your realtor's license suspended?

310

FRAN
I certainly did.

HOWARD
You wouldn't make such a mistake again, would you?

FRAN
It was no mistake, and when I get my license back I'll sell a house to another Negro the first chance I get. Madison needed rooms for Negro girl students and I was proud to sell that house to the Doxeys.

SARAH
Did you sell a house to a Negro family?

FRAN
Yes, I did.

HOWARD
In direct violation of the Realtor's Code of Ethics.

SARAH
Your code says you can't sell houses to Negroes?

HOWARD
Of course we can, where it's appropriate.

FRAN
The realtor's code is very clever and very sinister, in my opinion. It says a realtor should not sell a house if the buyer's race or the character of the occupancy would materially depreciate a neighborhood. Now please excuse me. My husband died in the war fighting for freedom and I need to do whatever I can to continue that fight.

311

Fran Remeika enters the Council Chamber.

SARAH
Are you prejudiced against Negroes?

HOWARD
Not at all, but other people are.

SARAH
Is that so. I bet you wouldn't want your daughter to marry one, would you, not even a rich one.

HOWARD
Don't you even think of such a thing!!!

SARAH
And you aren't prejudiced! I can't believe you said that.

HOWARD
I am not prejudiced. And the way you talk back to your elders is disgraceful. I hope you aren't this disrespectful in school.

SARAH
Don't worry. I'm not. I don't have to argue with people like you there.

HOWARD
Sarah, stop it!

Howard is again brought near to slapping her.

I don't want you in there!

SARAH
Don't worry.

312

HOWARD
I don't want people to think an Atwood is in favor of ... Are
you dating a Negro behind my back?

SARAH
No, I am not. I don't really even know any to talk to. But I
wish I did, just to make you go nuclear.

HOWARD
I have to go, or I'll be late.

Howard enters the chamber.

SARAH
He is so infuriating! *George and Edwin enter.* I wish I
could do something. I wish I could do something to oppose
him, without letting him know.

George puts his hands over Kate's eyes.

GEORGE
Hey, Kate, guess who.

KATE
Uh, Ted?

GEORGE
Ted?! I don't sound a bit like Ted.

KATE
I knew it was you, George. I was expecting you. This is
Sarah Atwood. She goes to West with me.

GEORGE
Fab! Hello. My name is George, like the Beatle.

SARAH

313

Hi.

GEORGE
And this is Ed Anderson. He goes to Central with me.

KATE and SARAH
Hi.

EDWIN
Hi.

GEORGE
Say, do you know how many City Council members it takes to change a light bulb?

SARAH
No.

GEORGE
None. One to say it needs to be changed. One from the opposing party to say it doesn't need to be changed. Then the usual song and dance, with half supporting the first side and half supporting the other, and while they're debating a point of order, the janitor changes it.

> *A photographer with an SLR and lots of lenses*
> *enters from the Council Chamber.*

GEORGE
So have they started yet?

KATE
I don't think so. There were a lot of things on the agenda before the Ordinance.

PHOTOGRAPHER
They're just finished voting down Frank Lloyd Wright's
Monona Terrace – again – and they're starting debate on the
Ordinance. Did any of you notice a pay phone around here?

KATE
Down the hall, next to the elevator.

PHOTOGRAPHER
Where?

EDWIN
I'll show you.

PHOTOGRAPHER
Thanks.

The Photographer follows Edwin off.

GEORGE
Did you watch the television special last night on the
assassination?

KATE
No, I couldn't. It's too painful.

GEORGE
Where were you when you heard the news.

SARAH
In German class. There was an announcement over the P.A.
system, "The President has been shot in Dallas. He died a
few minutes ago." Everything just stopped. Where were
you.

GEORGE

In gym class. We all just stopped what we were doing, and went to the showers. After school I went down to the recruiting station and got information about how to register for the draft when I turn eighteen.

SARAH
Why'd you do that.

GEORGE
I want to do my patriotic duty.

SARAH
But they might send you to Vietnam.

GEORGE
If my country calls, I'll go.

Edwin returns.

SARAH
But that's a stupid war. I read that the Vietnamese have been fighting for their freedom from colonial powers for hundreds of years – first the Chinese, then the Japanese, then the French, and now us.

GEORGE
We aren't colonizing them. We're fighting the commies.

SARAH *to Edwin*
What do you know about Vietnam.

EDWIN
Not much. Not as much as you do.

SARAH
Would you go to a foreign country and fight and kill people, and maybe get killed yourself, without knowing why?

316

EDWIN
I'm tryin' to make it here myself. Why would I want to go
kill people I don't know.

KATE
I was in study hall. We all just looked at each other, and
then I heard people crying. *To Edwin.* Where were you.

EDWIN
I was in history. We were quiet for a long time and then
Mister Thompson asked what we thought might happen.
Right now I'm wondering if the Civil Rights Act is dead.

GEORGE
Are you gonna go in and watch?

KATE
Yeah, let's go.

SARAH
I don't think so. My father's a real estate broker, and he's in
there, to speak on the wrong side. We already went a couple
of rounds just before you got here, and I don't need to
antagonize him any more. Who knows, it might give him
the critical mass he needs to rise to heights of eloquence, and
I wouldn't want that.

GEORGE
Let's go.

KATE
All right.

GEORGE
Ed?

317

EDWIN
In a minute. Save me a space if you can.

GEORGE
Copacetic.

George and Kate enter the chamber.

EDWIN
I think I saw you the other day.

SARAH
Oh? Where.

EDWIN
At Kehl Dance Studio. Was that you just signing up?

SARAH
Yes! Were you there?

EDWIN
Yeah.

SARAH
Do you dance there?

EDWIN
Yeah. I've been studying there about four years.

SARAH
You must be good.

EDWIN
Just trying to get better. I do get to dance a lot, but that's just because they never have enough guys. Maybe I'll see you there.

SARAH
I hope so. I bet you can actually do the twist. Not like the
guys I know.

EDWIN
Yeah. And the jerk.

SARAH
What do you think of the new Beatles song.

EDWIN
I want to hold your hand,   SARAH
I want to hold your hand.   I want to
hold your hand.

*She initiates dancing, which they do for just a few
moments before they get embarrassed.*

EDWIN
Actually, the reason I wanted to say something to you before
I go in and watch ... if your father's a bigwig in the real
estate world, what are you doing working for the ordinance.

SARAH
I told you, I'm not like him. I see his prejudice and I don't
want my world to be like that.

EDWIN
Did I hear you say you wanted to do something more to
help?

SARAH
Yeah. All I've been doing is handing out leaflets and talking
to people, mostly at school, kids who can't vote anyway.

EDWIN
There are a couple of young lawyers who helped draft the

319

ordinance. If it doesn't pass tonight, I was planning to see if they could use my help in some way.

SARAH
I'd be willing to do that. Who are they.

EDWIN
I just saw their names in the paper. They're with the La Follette firm: Gordon Sinykin and Shirley Abrahamson.

SARAH
I don't know them. Do you think it'll pass?

EDWIN
I don't know any more than you do. Are you asking me because the Negro will know?

SARAH
No! Of course not.

EDWIN
Why don't you go out on the street and ask Snowball Riley if he thinks it'll pass.

SARAH
I'm not like that. Really! But you'd hear different things, being at Central and all, and because you're a Negro. I should tell you I live in a house full of prejudice, but I try to be better. Do you know Snowball Riley? I've seen him, but I've never talked to him.

EDWIN
He's a character. No, I don't talk to him either. He's sort of an embarrassment. I see him washing windows when he needs money. But I heard he wasn't always like that. He got put in jail a long time ago and he just wasn't the same when he got out.

SARAH
Do you think all whites are prejudiced?

EDWIN
I think it's hard for whites not to be prejudiced in this
society.

SARAH
I hope I'm not. I hope I've learned to be tolerant of
everyone, except maybe the intolerant. I'd hate to be like my
father.

EDWIN
If prejudice means prejudging how a person's going to act
based just on skin color, maybe there's as much prejudice in
my house.

SARAH
Why is that. I mean, what with everything that goes on in
the South these days -- shootings, burnings, lynchings, civil
rights workers killed -- maybe you don't need a reason, but ...

EDWIN
Well, you know, racial violence isn't confined to the South.

SARAH
I know. Look at South Africa. But at least there hasn't been
any here.

EDWIN
Not quite right.

SARAH
What do you mean.

EDWIN

321

It's thirty-some years ago now, but my family knew the Hendersons.

SARAH
I'm sorry, should I know about the Hendersons?

EDWIN
I guess there's no reason for whites to repeat the story. They owned a farm on the south side of town and one day, for no apparent reason, they were murdered by a white man, Harvey Nelson. He cut the telephone lines to their house and shot Allen Henderson and his son Walter over a dozen times, and then when the police cornered him, he shot himself.

SARAH
Was he with the ... the Ku Klux Klan.

EDWIN
Nobody knows, but the Klan was active in Madison in the twenties and thirties. Of course they didn't just hate Negroes. They wanted to protect white America from Negroes, Catholics, Jews, immigrants, radicals, and evolutionists.

SARAH
I'm sorry to say, I never knew there were Negroes killed in Madison.

EDWIN
And if nobody knows about it, is it the same as if it never happened? What's history? Anyway, my family may be as prejudiced against white people as you ... as your father is against Negroes, but I have to say I think our expectations are usually met.

SARAH

But not always. That's the point. When you generalize about a group, you're unfair to some people because groups are made up of individuals, and people are different.

The photographer re-enters.

PHOTOGRAPHER
Have they started voting?

SARAH
We don't know.

EDWIN
Sorry.

The photographer goes into the Council Chamber.

EDWIN
My family's here tonight, too. My mother and father and grandmother. Granny's especially interested because she just lost her house to the Greenbush Redevelopment Project and she don't have noplace -- excuse me, I was hearing her speak there -- she can't find anyplace in Madison to even rent, let alone buy. I should probably get in there.

SARAH
I've heard good and bad things about that project. What's your opinion.

EDWIN
For me and everybody I know there, it's the systematic destruction of a community. I guess the houses and apartments they build'll be better quality, and some people'll call that progress, but there'll be nothing left of a neighborhood spirit that's been around for generations. Something irreplaceable will be lost. You might be

323

surprised to know my family's been in Madison a long time, probably longer than yours. *She gives him a questioning look but says nothing.* My great-grandfather William Anderson came here right after the Civil War. He joined a Wisconsin unit when it swept through Tennessee, and then he came back and worked for J.C. Gregory.

SARAH
Should I know that name?

EDWIN
Only if you study history. *Beat.* What's your name again?

SARAH
Sarah.

EDWIN
Your last name.

SARAH
Atwood.

EDWIN
Are you related to the Atwoods ... to David Atwood, the first editor of the Wisconsin State Journal?

SARAH
Yes. He was my great-grandfather.

EDWIN
Whoa! Then I was wrong about my family being here longer than yours. My great-grandfather probably knew yours.

SARAH
He did?

EDWIN
The Gregorys were close friends with the Atwoods a
hundred years ago.

SARAH
It's a small world.

EDWIN
Sometimes.

> *A cheer goes up. Kate and George come out of the
> chamber door. The photographer rushes out and
> off.*

KATE and GEORGE
It passed!

SARAH and EDWIN
It passed!

KATE
It was so exciting! You missed it! It was a tie vote, but
Mayor Reynolds broke the tie and voted <u>for</u> it!

> *Kate and George hug and jump up and down. Sarah
> and Edwin hug, stiffen up, then hug again. All four
> hug as others leave the chamber.*

SARAH
Papa will be in such a bad mood! He'll explode!

> *They all leave. Cross-fade. Lights down on scene 4
> and up in the attic.*

EPILOGUE

Holly is sitting on the floor just looking at an old photo. She looks up and is quiet for a minute. She puts the photos back very carefully and goes to the top of the stairs.

HOLLY
Mama.

The lights come up dimly in the living room as she descends.

Mama, is Daddy home yet?

EDWIN *[offstage]*
Yes, I just got home. I'll be there in a minute. Just let me clean up a little.

Edwin enters from one side as Sarah enters from the kitchen. He is wearing yet another topical tee-shirt. On opening night, this will be "Recall Mayor Dave". Edwin and Sarah kiss, lightly but not perfunctorily. Holly wrinkles her face in mock disgust.

SARAH
How are you.

EDWIN
I'm all right. I'm better. I ran down past Monona Terrace, and after about two miles I came to that park, you know, where all the soccer games are?

SARAH
Yes?

EDWIN
There was an adult soccer game, and they were so good I
stopped to watch. Almost everybody on both teams was
latino, from Mexico or some other country -- or I suppose
some of them could be native-born. The teams and the
spectators were talking mostly Spanish: "hombre!" "aqui!"
There were a couple of black guys on the teams. Maybe
they were Brazilian, who knows, but there was an anglo-
looking guy on one of the teams, and I noticed they didn't
pass to him much.

SARAH
Because he was white.

EDWIN
I don't know. Maybe he was having a bad day, or maybe he
was just a sub, or whatever, but …

SARAH
But?

EDWIN
Yeah, it looked like it was because he was white. And it
looked like the way I treat Martin.

SARAH
Yes?

EDWIN
Yeah. I saw Martin again as my son, as the little boy I had
to protect, as the kid I worked on math with, and I taught to
play soccer. I suddenly thought maybe I'm wrong. I've been
thinking about what our family was and what it will be, but
"was" and "will be" aren't "is". Today is. Martin isn't the
one breaking up the family. I am. Continuing the family's
important -- that hasn't changed -- but Martin is my family.
Who knows what will happen. I guess you can invite him

327

<u>and</u> his friend -- what's his name? --

HOLLY
Greg.

EDWIN
and Greg ... I may have trouble saying that ... and Greg home for your birthday.

HOLLY
Awesome, Daddy! Thank you!

She hugs him.

EDWIN
You're welcome.

He hugs and kisses Sarah. Holly wrinkles her nose and turns away.

HOLLY
Daddy, I've had the most exciting time, and I learned a lot about you and Mama I never knew!

SARAH
I let her look at some of our old photos, and as I was going through the trunk, look what I found!

EDWIN
What's that. We're on stage somewhere. What ridiculous costumes.

An opportunity for another projection.

SARAH
Don't you remember?

328

EDWIN
Wait! That's Shakespeare. Of course! "It is a tale told by an
idiot." That's "Mac --". I mean the Scottish play. No, it's
not. It's "Richard the Third". That was the first play we
were in together, wasn't it, with the Theatre Guild. "A horse!
A horse! My kingdom for a horse!"

SARAH
You've got the right play, but I was thinking more of

She takes his hand.

"Look how my ring encompasseth --

EDWIN
… encompasseth thy finger,
Even so thy breast encloseth my poor heart.
Wear both of them, for both of them are thine."
Our scene! Of course. No, I haven't forgotten.

He hugs her fondly.

HOLLY
Euw! Are you gonna get mushy?

EDWIN
Yeah. What are you gonna do about it.

HOLLY
Leave!

Holly starts to exit when Martin enters.

MARTIN
Hi. I came back 'cause I said I would.

SARAH, HOLLY and EDWIN simultaneously.

329

Martin!

MARTIN
Whoa. What did I miss.

Sarah and Holly look at Edwin.

EDWIN
Martin, I'd like to talk to you.

MARTIN
Uh-oh, are you gonna lecture me again about my "lifestyle"?

EDWIN
No. Not at all.

MARTIN
Don't, Dad. We had a nice day. We all got along together.
I left before anything upset you.

EDWIN
Well, I did get upset. After we saw all those families in the
cemetery --

MARTIN
Don't, Dad! Please. Let me just say "hi" and "good-bye" to
everybody and leave again.

EDWIN
No. That's not it --

MARTIN
Please! I know where this is leading.

EDWIN
No. It's about Holly's birthday party.

MARTIN
Okay? So?

EDWIN
After you left, I got upset, as I sometimes do, did, and I told Holly you couldn't come to her birthday party if you brought ... Greg.

MARTIN
That's it! I'm out of here!

He turns to walk out and Holly jumps up and stops him.

HOLLY
No. Wait. Really.

EDWIN
I've ... changed my mind. Maybe we can talk about it some more after we've both calmed down, but it would be okay with me if ... both of you came to her party.

Holly hugs him and Sarah goes over to him to put an arm around him.

MARTIN
Really?

EDWIN
Really.

MARTIN
Thanks, Dad.

HOLLY
I'm going to have the most awesome party ever. Can I have champagne?

331

MARTIN, EDWIN and SARAH
No!

> *Hugs all around. Lights down and curtain. Since
> this is community theatre, consider having the cast
> come forward into the audience after the final bow,
> instead of exiting backstage.*

CPSIA information can be obtained
at www.ICGtesting.com
Printed in the USA
LVHW052006110121
676217LV00009B/478

9 781087 937861